Second Edition

GREAT JOBS

FOR

D0596582

Theater Majors

Jan Goldberg

McGraw·Hill

New York   Chicago   San Francisco   Lisbon   London   Madrid   Mexico City
Milan   New Delhi   San Juan   Seoul   Singapore   Sydney   Toronto

Library of Congress Cataloging-in-Publication Data

Goldberg, Jan.
 Great jobs for theater majors / Jan Goldberg. — 2nd ed.
   p.   cm.
 Includes index.
 ISBN 0-07-143853-X (alk. paper)
 1. Theater—Vocational guidance.   I. Title.

 PN2074.G66   2004
 792.02'93—dc22   2004059968

2 3 4 5 6 7 8 9 0   DOC/DOC   0 9 8 7 6

ISBN 0-07-143853-X

McGraw-Hill books are available at special quantity discounts to use as premiums and sales promotions, or for use in corporate training programs. For more information, please write to the Director of Special Sales, Professional Publishing, McGraw-Hill, Two Penn Plaza, New York, NY 10121-2298. Or contact your local bookstore.

This book is printed on acid-free paper.

To my husband, Larry, for his continual love and support.
To my daughters, Sherri and Debbie, for always believing in me.
And to the memory of my father and mother, Sam and Sylvia Lefkovitz,
for encouraging me to follow my dreams.

Contents

Acknowledgments

The author gratefully acknowledges the professionals who graciously agreed to be profiled within and all of the associations and organizations that provided valuable and interesting information.

My dear husband, Larry; daughters, Sherri and Debbie; son-in-law Bruce; sister Adrienne; and brother, Paul; for their encouragement and support.

Family and close friends: Michele, Alison, Steven, Marty, Mindi, Cary, Michele, Marci, Steven, Brian, Jesse, Bertha, Aunt Estelle, Uncle Bernard, and Aunt Helen.

A special thanks to a special friend, Diana Catlin.

Sincere gratitude to Betsy Lancefield Lane, former editor at McGraw-Hill, for providing this challenging opportunity and help whenever and wherever it was needed.

Introduction

*"A just and lively image of human nature, representing its
passions and humors, and the changes of fortune to which it is subject,
for the delight and instruction of mankind."*
—JOHN DRYDEN

Acting as an art can be traced all the way back to the fifth century B.C.,
to the time of the early Greeks, who held contests for dramatists at religious festivals. In outdoor theaters, trained choruses sang or recited lines while
wearing masks symbolic of the emotions of anger, sorrow, fear, or joy. Some
of these plays, such as *Antigone* and *Oedipus Rex*, have lasted through time
and are still presented similarly today.

During the 1300s, dramas focusing on religious themes were presented
to provide a method of religious instruction. In the sixteenth century, the
Renaissance featured playwrights including Marlowe, who wrote *Doctor Faus-
tus*, Caleron, who wrote *Life Is a Dream*, and probably the most famous playwright of all, Shakespeare, who wrote *Hamlet, The Tempest, A Midsummer
Night's Dream, Romeo and Juliet, Julius Caesar*, and many others.

In the 1800s, theater in the United States advanced rapidly and several
dramatic groups were created, including the Washington Square Players and
the Provincetown Players. The early 1900s brought silent movies, a new and
exciting outlet for actors. Early performers in this medium included Charlie
Chaplin, Buster Keaton, and Mary Pickford.

When methods of recording sound were developed in 1926, actors were
allowed to speak as well as act. In the 1930s and 1940s, the heyday of radio
broadcasting, comic, musical, and dramatic presentations such as "The
Shadow," "The Jack Benny Show," "Fibber McGee and Molly," and "Amos
and Andy" were popular. This trend lasted only until the 1950s when television became the center of entertainment.

Today, performers may appear in dramas, comedies, musicals, commercials, and other types of presentations that may be seen in movies, on

television, or on the stage. These performances provide information, entertainment, education, and enrichment for millions of people living all over the world.

The Importance of Education

While it is true that having a college degree will not guarantee you a position in the world of theater (or any other field, for that matter), it is important to realize that this is the best way to prepare yourself and to increase your chances in the job market. No matter what specific career you choose, a higher education will:

1. Offer a broad base of knowledge and experiences
2. Allow you to increase and perfect your skills
3. Provide you with opportunities to gain important personal and professional contacts
4. Give you the information you need to make an informed career decision

Recognizing that there is intense competition, given the multitude of talented people vying for each job opening, you must somehow set yourself above and apart from the others. A dynamite combination is a college degree with at least one internship, additional formal training or study, experience working in the field, and enthusiasm along with a positive attitude. That's the way to truly position yourself with an edge over other well-qualified candidates.

Good luck in your quest!

PART ONE

THE JOB SEARCH

I

The Self-Assessment

Self-assessment is the process by which you begin to acknowledge your own particular blend of education, experiences, values, needs, and goals. It provides the foundation for career planning and the entire job search process. Self-assessment involves looking inward and asking yourself what can sometimes prove to be difficult questions. This self-examination should lead to an intimate understanding of your personal traits, your personal values, your consumption patterns and economic needs, your longer-term goals, your skill base, your preferred skills, and your underdeveloped skills.

You come to the self-assessment process knowing yourself well in some of these areas, but you may still be uncertain about other aspects. You may be well aware of your consumption patterns, but have you spent much time specifically identifying your longer-term goals or your personal values as they relate to work? No matter what level of self-assessment you have undertaken to date, it is now time to clarify all of these issues and questions as they relate to the job search.

The knowledge you gain in the self-assessment process will guide the rest of your job search. In this book, you will learn about all of the following tasks:

- Writing résumés and cover letters
- Researching careers and networking
- Interviewing and job offer considerations

In each of these steps, you will rely on and often return to the understanding gained through your self-assessment. Any individual seeking employment must be able and willing to express these facets of his or her personality to recruiters and interviewers throughout the job search. This communication allows you to show the world who you are so that together with employers you can determine whether there will be a workable match with a given job or career path.

How to Conduct a Self-Assessment

The self-assessment process goes on naturally all the time. People ask you to clarify what you mean, you make a purchasing decision, or you begin a new relationship. You react to the world and the world reacts to you. How you understand these interactions and any changes you might make because of them are part of the natural process of self-discovery. There is, however, a more comprehensive and efficient way to approach self-assessment with regard to employment.

Because self-assessment can become a complex exercise, we have distilled it into a seven-step process that provides an effective basis for undertaking a job search. The seven steps include the following:

1. Understanding your personal traits
2. Identifying your personal values
3. Calculating your economic needs
4. Exploring your longer-term goals
5. Enumerating your skill base
6. Recognizing your preferred skills
7. Assessing skills needing further development

As you work through your self-assessment, you might want to create a worksheet similar to the one shown in Exhibit 1.1, starting on the following page. Or you might want to keep a journal of the thoughts you have as you undergo this process. There will be many opportunities to revise your self-assessment as you start down the path of seeking a career.

Step 1   Understand Your Personal Traits
Each person has a unique personality that he or she brings to the job search process. Gaining a better understanding of your personal traits can help you evaluate job and career choices. Identifying these traits and then finding employment that allows you to draw on at least some of them can create a rewarding and fulfilling work experience. If potential employment doesn't allow you to use these preferred traits, it is important to decide whether you

Exhibit 1.1
SELF-ASSESSMENT WORKSHEET

Step 1. Understand Your Personal Traits
  The personal traits that describe me are:
  (Include all of the words that describe you.)
  The ten personal traits that most accurately describe me are:
  (List these ten traits.)

Step 2. Identify Your Personal Values
  Working conditions that are important to me include:
  (List working conditions that would have to exist for you to accept a position.)
  The values that go along with my working conditions are:
  (Write down the values that correspond to each working condition.)
  Some additional values I've decided to include are:
  (List those values you identify as you conduct this job search.)

Step 3. Calculate Your Economic Needs
  My estimated minimum annual salary requirement is:
  (Write the salary you have calculated based on your budget.)
  Starting salaries for the positions I'm considering are:
  (List the name of each job you are considering and the associated starting salary.)

Step 4. Explore Your Longer-Term Goals
  My thoughts on longer-term goals right now are:
  (Jot down some of your longer-term goals as you know them right now.)

Step 5. Enumerate Your Skill Base
  The general skills I possess are:
  (List the skills that underlie tasks you are able to complete.)
  The specific skills I possess are:
  (List more technical or specific skills that you possess, and indicate your level of expertise.)
  General and specific skills that I want to promote to employers for the jobs I'm considering are:
  (List general and specific skills for each type of job you are considering.)

continued

Step 6. Recognize Your Preferred Skills

Skills that I would like to use on the job include:

(List skills that you hope to use on the job, and indicate how often you'd like to use them.)

Step 7. Assess Skills Needing Further Development

Some skills that I'll need to acquire for the jobs I'm considering include:

(Write down skills listed in job advertisements or job descriptions that you don't currently possess.)

I believe I can build these skills by:

(Describe how you plan to acquire these skills.)

---

can find other ways to express them or whether you would be better off not considering this type of job. Interests and hobbies pursued outside of work hours can be one way to use personal traits you don't have an opportunity to draw on in your work. For example, if you consider yourself an outgoing person and the kinds of jobs you are examining allow little contact with other people, you may be able to achieve the level of interaction that is comfortable for you outside of your work setting. If such a compromise seems impractical or otherwise unsatisfactory, you probably should explore only jobs that provide the interaction you want and need on the job.

Many young adults who are not very confident about their employability will downplay their need for income. They will say, "Money is not all that important if I love my work." But if you begin to document exactly what you need for housing, transportation, insurance, clothing, food, and utilities, you will begin to understand that some jobs cannot meet your financial needs and it doesn't matter how wonderful the job is. If you have to worry each payday about bills and other financial obligations, you won't be very effective on the job. Begin now to be honest with yourself about your needs.

Begin the self-assessment process by creating an inventory of your personal traits. Make a list of as many words as possible to describe yourself. Words like *accurate, creative, future-oriented, relaxed,* or *structured* are just a few examples. In addition, you might ask people who know you well how they might describe you.

Focus on Selected Personal Traits. Of all the traits you identified, select the ten you believe most accurately describe you. Keep track of these ten traits.

Consider Your Personal Traits in the Job Search Process. As you begin exploring jobs and careers, watch for matches between your personal traits and the job descriptions you read. Some jobs will require many personal traits you know you possess, and others will not seem to match those traits.

For example, you might be interested in working as a drama teacher. Do the job requirements match your personal traits? Teaching drama will call upon your creativity and motivational skills. Since teaching is essentially outer-directed, your ability to create methods to stimulate, encourage, and guide students will be far more important personal traits for success than attention to your own technique and stage presence. As a teacher, you must be able to motivate and inspire others and to support their efforts without being overly critical or judgmental. All drama teachers must be sensitive to the needs and goals of their students. Those working within a school system must also be able to fulfill established curriculum requirements.

Your ability to respond to changing conditions, your decision-making ability, productivity, creativity, and verbal skills all have a bearing on your success in and enjoyment of your work life. To better guarantee success, be sure to take the time needed to understand these traits in yourself.

Step 2   Identify Your Personal Values

Your personal values affect every aspect of your life, including employment, and they develop and change as you move through life. Values can be defined as principles that we hold in high regard, qualities that are important and desirable to us. Some values aren't ordinarily connected to work (love, beauty, color, light, relationships, family, or religion), and others are (autonomy, cooperation, effectiveness, achievement, knowledge, and security). Our values determine, in part, the level of satisfaction we feel in a particular job.

Define Acceptable Working Conditions. One facet of employment is the set of working conditions that must exist for someone to consider taking a job.

Each of us would probably create a unique list of acceptable working conditions, but items that might be included on many people's lists are the amount of money you would need to be paid, how far you are willing to drive or travel, the amount of freedom you want in determining your own schedule, whether you would be working with people or data or things, and the types of tasks you would be willing to do. Your conditions might include statements of working conditions you will *not* accept; for example, you might not be willing to work at night or on weekends or holidays.

If you were offered a job tomorrow, what conditions would have to exist for you to realistically consider accepting the position? Take some time and make a list of these conditions.

Realize Associated Values. Your list of working conditions can be used to create an inventory of your values relating to jobs and careers you are exploring. For example, if one of your conditions stated that you wanted to earn at least $30,000 per year, the associated value would be financial gain. If another condition was that you wanted to work with a friendly group of people, the value that went along with that might be belonging or interaction with people.

Relate Your Values to the World of Work. As you read the job descriptions you come across either in this book, in newspapers and magazines, or online, think about the values associated with each position.

For example, the duties of a theatrical agent would include networking, investigating, and arranging auditions; coordinating schedules with producers and performers; fielding offers; and negotiating contracts. Associated values are organization, mobility, communication, and cooperation.

At least some of the associated values in the field you're exploring should match those you extracted from your list of working conditions. Take a second look at any values that don't match up. How important are they to you? What will happen if they are not satisfied on the job? Can you incorporate those personal values elsewhere? Your answers need to be brutally honest. As you continue your exploration, be sure to add to your list any additional values that occur to you.

Step 3 Calculate Your Economic Needs
Each of us grew up in an environment that provided for certain basic needs, such as food and shelter, and, to varying degrees, other needs that we now consider basic, such as cable television, e-mail, or an automobile. Needs such

as privacy, space, and quiet, which at first glance may not appear to be monetary needs, may add to housing expenses and so should be considered as you examine your economic needs. For example, if you place a high value on a large, open living space for yourself, it would be difficult to satisfy that need without an associated high housing cost, especially in a densely populated city environment.

As you prepare to move into the world of work and become responsible for meeting your own basic needs, it is important to consider the salary you will need to be able to afford a satisfying standard of living. The three-step process outlined here will help you plan a budget, which in turn will allow you to evaluate the various career choices and geographic locations you are considering. The steps include (1) developing a realistic budget, (2) examining starting salaries, and (3) using a cost-of-living index.

Develop a Realistic Budget. Each of us has certain expectations for the kind of lifestyle we want to maintain. To begin the process of defining your economic needs, it will be helpful to determine what you expect to spend on routine monthly expenses. These expenses include housing, food, transportation, entertainment, utilities, loan repayments, and revolving charge accounts. You may not currently spend anything for certain items, but you probably will have to once you begin supporting yourself. As you develop this budget, be generous in your estimates, but keep in mind any items that could be reduced or eliminated. If you are not sure about the cost of a certain item, talk with family or friends who would be able to give you a realistic estimate.

If this is new or difficult for you, start to keep a log of expenses right now. You may be surprised at how much you actually spend each month for food or stamps or magazines. Household expenses and personal grooming items can often loom very large in a budget, as can auto repairs or home maintenance.

Income taxes must also be taken into consideration when examining salary requirements. State and local taxes vary, so it is difficult to calculate exactly the effect of taxes on the amount of income you need to generate. To roughly estimate the gross income necessary to generate your minimum annual salary requirement, multiply the minimum salary you have calculated by a factor of 1.35. The resulting figure will be an approximation of what your gross income would need to be, given your estimated expenses.

Examine Starting Salaries. Starting salaries for each of the career tracks are provided throughout this book. These salary figures can be used in conjunction with the cost-of-living index (discussed in the next section) to determine whether you would be able to meet your basic economic needs in a given geographic location.

Use a Cost-of-Living Index. If you are thinking about trying to get a job in a geographic region other than the one where you now live, understanding differences in the cost of living will help you come to a more informed decision about making a move. By using a cost-of-living index, you can compare salaries offered and the cost of living in different locations with what you know about the salaries offered and the cost of living in your present location.

Many variables are used to calculate the cost-of-living index. Often included are housing, groceries, utilities, transportation, health care, clothing, and entertainment expenses. Right now you do not need to worry about the details associated with calculating a given index. The main purpose of this exercise is to help you understand that pay ranges for entry-level positions may not vary greatly, but the cost of living in different locations *can* vary tremendously.

If you lived in Cleveland, Ohio, for example, and you were interested in working as a high school drama teacher in the Cleveland School District, you would earn, on average, $28,600 annually. But let's say you're also thinking about moving to New York, Los Angeles, or Minneapolis. You know you can live on $28,600 in Cleveland, but you want to be able to equate that salary in other locations you're considering.

JOB: HIGH SCHOOL DRAMA TEACHER

City	Index	Equivalent Salary
New York	213.3	
		× $28,600 = $53,482 in New York
	114.3	
Los Angeles	124.6	
		× $28,600 = $31,174 in Los Angeles
	114.3	
Minneapolis	100.0	
		× $28,600 = $24,882 in Minneapolis
	114.3	

You would have to earn $53,482 in New York, $31,174 in Los Angeles, and $24,882 in Minneapolis to match the buying power of $28,600 in Cleveland.

If you would like to determine whether it's financially worthwhile to make any of these moves, one more piece of information is needed: the salaries of high school drama teachers in these other cities. Average salary information for secondary school teachers in the 2002–2003 year were:

Region	Annual Salary	Salary Equivalent to Ohio	Change in Buying Power
Mid-Atlantic (including New York)	$35,259	$53,482	−$18,223
West (including Los Angeles)	$34,805	$31,174	+$3,631
Great Plains (including Minneapolis)	$24,882	$28,866	+$266
Midwest (including Cleveland)	$28,600	—	—

If you moved to New York City and secured employment as a high school drama teacher, you would not be able to maintain a lifestyle similar to the one you led in Cleveland; in fact, you would have to add more than 50 percent to your income to maintain a similar lifestyle in New York. The same would not be true for a move to Los Angeles or Minneapolis. You would increase your buying power given the rate of pay and cost of living in these cities.

You can work through a similar exercise for any type of job you are considering and for many locations when current salary information is available. It will be worth your time to undertake this analysis if you are seriously considering a relocation. By doing so you will be able to make an informed choice.

Step 4 Explore Your Longer-Term Goals

There is no question that when we first begin working, our goals are to use our skills and education in a job that will reward us with employment, income, and status relative to the preparation we brought with us to this position. If we are not being paid as much as we feel we should for our level of education or if job demands don't provide the intellectual stimulation we had hoped for, we experience unhappiness and as a result often seek other employment.

Most jobs we consider "good" are those that fulfill our basic "lower-level" needs of security, food, clothing, shelter, income, and productive work. But even when our basic needs are met and our jobs are secure and productive, we as individuals are constantly changing. As we change, the demands and expectations we place on our jobs may change. Fortunately, some jobs grow and change with us, and this explains why some people are happy throughout many years in a job.

But more often people are bigger than the jobs they fill. We have more goals and needs than any job could satisfy. These are "higher-level" needs of self-esteem, companionship, affection, and an increasing desire to feel we are employing ourselves in the most effective way possible. Not all of these higher-level needs can be met through employment, but for as long as we are employed, we increasingly demand that our jobs play their part in moving us along the path to fulfillment.

Another obvious but important fact is that we change as we mature. Although our jobs also have the potential for change, they may not change as frequently or as markedly as we do. There are increasingly fewer one-job, one-employer careers; we must think about a work future that may involve voluntary or forced moves from employer to employer. Because of that very real possibility, we need to take advantage of the opportunities in each position we hold. Acquiring the skills and competencies associated with each position will keep us viable and attractive as employees. This is particularly true in a job market that not only is technology/computer dependent, but also is populated with more and more small, self-transforming organizations rather than the large, seemingly stable organizations of the past.

For instance, if you are considering a career as an actor, you would gain valuable insight by talking with people who work as actors in different settings. Actors who work on stage, in films, in television, and in commercials and videos will all have different perspectives, opinions, and suggestions that might help you to decide if this is the best career for you.

Step 5   Enumerate Your Skill Base

In terms of the job search, skills can be thought of as capabilities that can be developed in school, at work, or by volunteering and then used in specific job settings. Many studies have documented the kinds of skills that employers seek in entry-level applicants. For example, some of the most desired skills for individuals interested in the teaching profession are the ability to interact effectively with students one-on-one, to manage a classroom, to adapt to varying situations as necessary, and to get involved in school activities. Business employers have also identified important qualities, including enthusiasm for the employer's product or service, a businesslike mind, the ability to follow written or oral instructions, the ability to demonstrate self-control, the confidence to suggest new ideas, the ability to communicate with all members of a group, an awareness of cultural differences, and loyalty, to name just a few. You will find that many of these skills are also in the repertoire of qualities demanded in your college major.

To be successful in obtaining any given job, you must be able to demonstrate that you possess a certain mix of skills that will allow you to carry out the duties required by that job. This skill mix will vary a great deal from job to job; to determine the skills necessary for the jobs you are seeking, you can read job advertisements or more generic job descriptions, such as those found later in this book. If you want to be effective in the job search, you must directly show employers that you possess the skills needed to be successful in filling the position. These skills will initially be described on your résumé and then discussed again during the interview process.

Skills are either general or specific. To develop a list of skills relevant to employers, you must first identify the general skills you possess, then list specific skills you have to offer, and, finally, examine which of these skills employers are seeking.

Identify Your General Skills. Because you possess or will possess a college degree, employers will assume that you can read and write, perform certain basic computations, think critically, and communicate effectively. Employers will want to see that you have acquired these skills, and they will want to know which additional general skills you possess.

One way to begin identifying skills is to write an experiential diary. An experiential diary lists all the tasks you were responsible for completing for each job you've held and then outlines the skills required to do those tasks. You may list several skills for any given task. This diary allows you to distinguish between the tasks you performed and the underlying skills required to complete those tasks. (See example at the top of page 14.)

For each job or experience you have participated in, develop a worksheet based on the example shown here. On a résumé, you may want to describe these skills rather than simply listing tasks. Skills are easier for the employer to appreciate, especially when your experience is very different from the

Tasks	Skills
Answering telephone	Effective use of language, clear diction, ability to direct inquiries, ability to solve problems
Waiting on tables	Poise under conditions of time and pressure, speed, accuracy, good memory, simultaneous completion of tasks, sales skills

employment you are seeking. In addition to helping you identify general skills, this experiential diary will prepare you to speak more effectively in an interview about the qualifications you possess.

Identify Your Specific Skills. It may be easier to identify your specific skills because you can definitely say whether you can speak other languages, program a computer, draft a map or diagram, or edit a document using appropriate symbols and terminology.

Using your experiential diary, identify the points in your history where you learned how to do something very specific, and decide whether you have a beginning, intermediate, or advanced knowledge of how to use that particular skill. Right now, be sure to list *every* specific skill you have, and don't consider whether you like using the skill. Write down a list of specific skills you have acquired and the level of competence you possess—beginning, intermediate, or advanced.

Relate Your Skills to Employers. You probably have thought about a couple of different jobs you might be interested in obtaining, and one way to begin relating the general and specific skills you possess to a potential employer's needs is to read actual advertisements for these types of positions (see Part Two for resources listing actual job openings).

For example, you might be interested in a career as a broadcast technician. A typical job listing might read, "Requires 2–5 years experience, organizational and interpersonal skills, imagination, drive, and the ability to work under pressure." If you then used any one of a number of general sources of information that describe the job of a broadcast technician, you would find additional information. Broadcast technicians also install, test, repair, set up, and operate the electronic equipment used to record and transmit radio and television programs. They work with television cameras, microphones, tape recorders, transmitters, antennas, and other equipment.

Begin building a comprehensive list of required skills with the first job description you read. Exploring advertisements for and descriptions of several types of related positions will reveal an important core of skills necessary for obtaining the type of work you're interested in. In building this list, include both general and specific skills.

Following is a sample list of skills needed to be successful as a broadcast technician. These items were extracted from general resources and actual job listings.

JOB: BROADCAST TECHNICIAN

General Skills	Specific Skills
Have a specific body of knowledge	Be proficient with electronics
Work long hours near deadline	Be familiar with control rooms
Work well with other people	Work with transmitters
Be able to work under pressure	Test equipment functions
Have physical stamina	Operate television cameras
Possess manual dexterity	Set up sound effects

On separate sheets of paper, try to generate a comprehensive list of required skills for at least one job you are considering.

The list of general skills that you develop for a given career path would be valuable for any number of jobs you might apply for. Many of the specific skills would also be transferable to other types of positions. For example, broadcast technicians who work with television transmitters and antennas would utilize many of the same skills working in radio stations.

Step 6 Recognize Your Preferred Skills

In the previous section you developed a comprehensive list of skills that relate to particular career paths that are of interest to you. You can now relate these to skills that you prefer to use. We all use a wide range of skills (some researchers say individuals have a repertoire of about five hundred skills), but we may not particularly be interested in using all of them in our work. There may be some skills that come to us more naturally or that we use success-fully time and time again and that we want to continue to use; these are best described as our preferred skills. For this exercise use the list of skills that you created for the previous section, and decide which of them you are *most interested in using* in future work and how often you would like to use them. You might be interested in using some skills only occasionally, while others you would like to use more regularly. You probably also have skills that you hope you can use constantly.

As you examine job announcements, look for matches between this list of preferred skills and the qualifications described in the advertisements. These skills should be highlighted on your résumé and discussed in job interviews.

Step 7 Assess Skills Needing Further Development

Previously you compiled a list of general and specific skills required for given positions. You already possess some of these skills; those that remain to be developed are your underdeveloped skills.

If you are just beginning the job search, there may be gaps between the qualifications required for some of the jobs you're considering and the skills you possess. The thought of having to admit to and talk about these under-developed skills, especially in a job interview, is a frightening one. One way to put a healthy perspective on this subject is to target and relate your explo-ration of underdeveloped skills to the types of positions you are seeking. Rec-ognizing these shortcomings and planning to overcome them with either on-the-job training or additional formal education can be a positive way to address the concept of underdeveloped skills.

On your worksheet or in your journal, make a list of up to five general or specific skills required for the positions you're interested in that you *don't currently possess*. For each item list an idea you have for specific action you could take to acquire that skill. Do some brainstorming to come up with possible actions. If you have a hard time generating ideas, talk to people cur-rently working in this type of position, professionals in your college career services office, trusted friends, family members, or members of related pro-fessional associations.

In the chapter on interviewing, we will discuss in detail how to effectively address questions about underdeveloped skills. Generally speaking, though, employers want genuine answers to these types of questions. They want you to reveal "the real you," and they also want to see how you answer difficult questions. In taking the positive, targeted approach discussed previously, you show the employer that you are willing to continue to learn and that you have a plan for strengthening your job qualifications.

Use Your Self-Assessment

Exploring entry-level career options can be an exciting experience if you have good resources available and will take the time to use them. Can you effectively complete the following tasks?

1. Understand your personality traits and relate them to career choices
2. Define your personal values
3. Determine your economic needs
4. Explore longer-term goals
5. Understand your skill base
6. Recognize your preferred skills
7. Express a willingness to improve on your underdeveloped skills

If so, then you can more meaningfully participate in the job search process by writing a more effective résumé, finding job titles that represent work you are interested in doing, locating job sites that will provide the opportunity for you to use your strengths and skills, networking in an informed way, participating in focused interviews, getting the most out of follow-up contacts, and evaluating job offers to find those that create a good match between you and the employer. The remaining chapters in Part One guide you through these next steps in the job search process. For many job seekers, this process can take anywhere from three months to a year to implement. The time you will need to put into your job search will depend on the type of job you want and the geographic location where you'd like to work. Think of your effort as a job in itself, requiring you to set aside time each week to complete the needed work. Carefully undertaken efforts may reduce the time you need for your job search.

2

The Résumé and Cover Letter

The task of writing a résumé may seem overwhelming if you are unfamiliar with this type of document, but there are some easily understood techniques that can and should be used. This section was written to help you understand the purpose of the résumé, the different types of résumé formats available, and how to write the sections of information traditionally found on a résumé. We will present examples and explanations that address questions frequently posed by people writing their first résumé or updating an old résumé.

Even within the formats and suggestions given, however, there are infinite variations. True, most résumés follow one of the outlines suggested, but you should feel free to adjust the résumé to suit your needs and make it expressive of your life and experience.

Why Write a Résumé?

The purpose of a résumé is to convince an employer that you should be interviewed. Whether you're mailing, faxing, or e-mailing this document, you'll want to present enough information to show that you can make an immediate and valuable contribution to an organization. A résumé is not an in-depth historical or legal document; later in the job search process you may be asked to document your entire work history on an application form and attest to its validity. The résumé should, instead, highlight relevant information pertaining directly to the organization that will receive the document or to the type of position you are seeking.

We will discuss the chronological and digital résumés in detail here. Functional and targeted résumés, which are used much less often, are briefly discussed. The reasons for using one type of résumé over another and the typical format for each are addressed in the following sections.

The Chronological Résumé

The chronological résumé is the most common of the various résumé formats and therefore the format that employers are most used to receiving. This type of résumé is easy to read and understand because it details the chronological progression of jobs you have held. (See Exhibit 2.1.) It begins with your most recent employment and works back in time. If you have a solid work history or have experience that provided growth and development in your duties and responsibilities, a chronological résumé will highlight these achievements. The typical elements of a chronological résumé include the heading, a career objective, educational background, employment experience, activities, and references.

The Heading
The heading consists of your name, address, telephone number, and other means of contact. This may include a fax number, e-mail address, and your home-page address. If you are using a shared e-mail account or a parent's business fax, be sure to let others who use these systems know that you may receive important professional correspondence via these systems. You wouldn't want to miss a vital e-mail or fax! Likewise, if your résumé directs readers to a personal home page on the Web, be certain it's a professional personal home page designed to be viewed and appreciated by a prospective employer. This may mean making substantial changes in the home page you currently mount on the Web.

The Objective
Without a doubt the objective statement is the most challenging part of the résumé for most writers. Even for individuals who have decided on a career path, it can be difficult to encapsulate all they want to say in one or two brief sentences. For job seekers who are unfocused or unclear about their intentions, trying to write this section can inhibit the entire résumé writing process.

Keep the objective as short as possible and no longer than two short sentences.

Exhibit 2.1
CHRONOLOGICAL RÉSUMÉ

JEFFREY GORDON

Hampton House #450
UCLA
3400 Michigan Avenue
Los Angeles, CA 90025
(213) 555-4334
(until June 2005)

2502 Victoria Street
Santa Barbara, CA 93105
(805) 555-0987

OBJECTIVE
A career as a staff writer in television or films

EDUCATION
Bachelor of Arts in Film
UCLA
Los Angeles, California
June 2005

RELATED COURSES
Creative Writing
Computer Graphics
Film History
Desktop Publishing

EXPERIENCE
Work-Study
Atlantic Productions
Santa Monica, California
Reader, Office Assistant
2003 to present
Read and reported on screenplays submitted for production; performed general
    office duties, answered phone, filed, scheduled appointments.

Internships
Universal Studios
Orlando, Florida
2003 to 2004

continued

Assistant to the Creative Director
Worked on developing scripts for Nickelodeon
   broadcasts.

Table of Content Café
Los Angeles, California
Summers, 2002–2004
Waited tables.

PUBLICATIONS
Short stories and poems published in a variety of literary magazines. Sample TV
   scripts and screenplays are available upon request.

REFERENCES
Both personal and professional references are available upon request.

Choose one of the following types of objective statement:

1. *General Objective Statement*

- An entry-level educational programming coordinator position

2. *Position-Focused Objective*

- To obtain the position of conference coordinator at State College

3. *Industry-Focused Objective*

- To begin a career as a sales representative in the cruise line industry

4. *Summary of Qualifications Statement*

A graduate degree in psychology combined with a bachelor's
degree in theater arts, and three years of experience working in
a children's hospital have prepared me for a career as a full-time
drama therapist in an institution that values hands-on involvement
and creativity.

Support Your Objective. A résumé that contains any one of these types of objective statements should then go on to demonstrate why you are qualified to get the position. Listing academic degrees can be one way to indicate qualifications. Another demonstration would be in the way previous experiences, both volunteer and paid, are described. Without this kind of documentation in the body of the résumé, the objective looks unsupported. Think of the résumé as telling a connected story about you. All the elements should work together to form a coherent picture that ideally should relate to your statement of objective.

Education

This section of your résumé should indicate the exact name of the degree you will receive or have received, spelled out completely with no abbreviations. The degree is generally listed after the objective, followed by the institution name and location, and then the month and year of graduation. This section could also include your academic minor, grade point average (GPA), and appearance on the Dean's List or President's List.

If you have enough space, you might want to include a section listing courses related to the field in which you are seeking work. The best use of a "related courses" section would be to list some course work that is not traditionally associated with the major. Perhaps you took several computer courses outside your degree that will be helpful and related to the job prospects you are entertaining. Several education section examples are shown here:

- Bachelor of Arts degree in theater arts, UCLA, Los Angeles, California, May 2005, Minor: English
- Bachelor of Arts degree in drama, Tufts University, Medford, Massachusetts, May 2004, Minor: Screenwriting
- Bachelor of Science degree in broadcast technology, State University, Boulder Colorado, 2004, Minor: Music

An example of a format for a related-courses section follows:

RELATED COURSES	
Creative Writing	Computer Graphics
Economics	Art History
Technical Writing	Desktop Publishing

Experience

The experience section of your résumé should be the most substantial part and should take up most of the space on the page. Employers want to see what kind of work history you have. They will look at your range of experiences, longevity in jobs, and specific tasks you are able to complete. This section may also be called "work experience," "related experience," "employment history," or "employment." No matter what you call this section, some important points to remember are the following:

1. **Describe your duties** as they relate to the position you are seeking.
2. **Emphasize major responsibilities** and indicate increases in responsibility. Include all relevant employment experiences: summer, part-time, internships, cooperative education, or self-employment.
3. **Emphasize skills**, especially those that transfer from one situation to another. The fact that you coordinated a student organization, chaired meetings, supervised others, and managed a budget leads one to suspect that you could coordinate other things as well.
4. **Use descriptive job titles** that provide information about what you did. A "Student Intern" should be more specifically stated as, for example, "Magazine Operations Intern." "Volunteer" is also too general; a title such as "Peer Writing Tutor" would be more appropriate.
5. **Create word pictures** by using active verbs to start sentences. Describe *results* you have produced in the work you have done.

A limp description would say something such as the following: "My duties included helping with production, proofreading, and editing. I used a design and page layout program." An action statement would be stated as follows: "Coordinated and assisted in the creative marketing of brochures and seminar promotions, becoming proficient in Quark."

Remember, an accomplishment is simply a result, a final measurable product that people can relate to. A duty is not a result; it is an obligation—every job holder has duties. For an effective résumé, list as many results as you can. To make the most of the limited space you have and to give your description impact, carefully select appropriate and accurate descriptors.

Here are some traits that employers tell us they like to see:

- Teamwork
- Energy and motivation
- Learning and using new skills

- Versatility
- Critical thinking
- Understanding how profits are created
- Organizational acumen
- Communicating directly and clearly, in both writing and speaking
- Risk taking
- Willingness to admit mistakes
- High personal standards

Solutions to Frequently Encountered Problems

Repetitive Employment with the Same Employer

EMPLOYMENT: The Foot Locker, Portland, Oregon. Summer 2001, 2002, 2003. Initially employed in high school as salesclerk. Due to successful performance, asked to return next two summers at higher pay with added responsibility. Ranked as the #2 salesperson the first summer and #1 the next two summers. Assisted in arranging eye-catching retail displays; served as manager of other summer workers during owner's absence.

A Large Number of Jobs

EMPLOYMENT: Recent Hospitality Industry Experience: Affiliated with four upscale hotel/restaurant complexes (September 2001–February 2004), where I worked part- and full-time as a waiter, bartender, disc jockey, and bookkeeper to produce income for college.

Several Positions with the Same Employer

EMPLOYMENT: Coca-Cola Bottling Co., Burlington, Vermont, 2001–2004. In four years, I received three promotions, each with increased pay and responsibility.

Summer Sales Coordinator: Promoted to hire, train, and direct efforts of add-on staff of fifteen college-age route salespeople hired to meet summer peak demand for product.

Sales Administrator: Promoted to run home office sales desk, managing accounts and associated delivery schedules for professional sales force of ten people. Intensive phone work, daily interaction with all personnel, and strong knowledge of product line required.

Route Salesperson: Summer employment to travel and tourism industry sites that use Coke products. Met specific schedule demands, used good communication skills with wide variety of customers, and demonstrated strong selling skills. Named salesperson of the month for July of that year.

Questions Résumé Writers Often Ask

How Far Back Should I Go in Terms of Listing Past Jobs?

Usually, listing three or four jobs should suffice. If you did something back in high school that has a bearing on your future aspirations for employment, by all means list the job. As you progress through your college career, high school jobs will be replaced on the résumé by college employment.

Should I Differentiate Between Paid and Nonpaid Employment?

Most employers are not initially concerned about how much you were paid. They are anxious to know how much responsibility you held in your past employment. There is no need to specify that your work was as a volunteer if you had significant responsibilities.

How Should I Represent My Accomplishments or Work-Related Responsibilities?

Succinctly, but fully. In other words, give the employer enough information to arouse curiosity but not so much detail that you leave nothing to the imagination. Besides, some jobs merit more lengthy explanations than others. Be sure to convey any information that can give an employer a better understanding of the depth of your involvement at work. Did you supervise others? How many? Did your efforts result in a more efficient operation? How much did you increase efficiency? Did you handle a budget? How much? Were you promoted in a short time? Did you work two jobs at once or fifteen hours per week after high school? Where appropriate, quantify.

Should the Work Section Always Follow the Education Section on the Résumé?

Always lead with your strengths. If your education closely relates to the employment you now seek, put this section after the objective. If your education does not closely relate but you have a surplus of good work experiences, consider reversing the order of your sections to lead with employment, followed by education.

How Should I Present My Activities, Honors, Awards, Professional Societies, and Affiliations?

This section of the résumé can add valuable information for an employer to consider if used correctly. The rule of thumb for information in this section is to include only those activities that are in some way relevant to the objective stated on your résumé. If you are able to draw a valid connection between your activities and your objective, include them; if not, leave them out.

Professional affiliations and honors should all be listed; especially important are those related to your job objective. Social clubs and activities need not be a part of your résumé unless you hold a significant office or you are looking for a position related to your membership. Be aware that most prospective employers' principal concerns are related to your employability, not your social life. If you have any, publications can be included as an addendum to your résumé.

How Should I Handle References?

The use of references is considered a part of the interview process, and they should never be listed specifically on a résumé. You would always provide references to a potential employer if requested to, so it is not even necessary to include this section on the résumé if space does not permit. If enough space is available, it is acceptable to include a statement such as the following example:

- REFERENCES:
  Furnished upon request.

The Functional Résumé

The functional résumé departs from a chronological résumé in that it organizes information by specific accomplishments in various settings: previous jobs, volunteer work, associations, and so forth. This type of résumé permits you to stress the substance of your experiences rather than the position titles you have held. You should consider using a functional résumé if you have held a series of similar jobs that relied on the same skills or abilities. There are many good books in which you can find examples of functional résumés, including *How to Write a Winning Resume* or *Resumes Made Easy*.

The Targeted Résumé

The targeted résumé focuses on specific work-related capabilities you can bring to a given position within an organization. Past achievements are listed to highlight your capabilities and the work history section is abbreviated.

Digital Résumés

Today's employers have to manage an enormous number of résumés. One of the most frequent complaints the writers of this series hear from students is the failure of employers to even acknowledge the receipt of a résumé and cover letter. Frequently, the reason for this poor response or nonresponse is the volume of applications received for every job. In an attempt to better manage the considerable labor investment involved in processing large numbers of résumés, many employers are requiring digital submission of résumés. There are two types of digital résumés: those that can be e-mailed or posted to a website, called *electronic résumés*, and those that can be "read" by a computer, commonly called *scannable résumés*. Though the format may be a bit different from the traditional "paper" résumé, the goal of both types of digital résumés is the same—to get you an interview! These résumés must be designed to be "technologically friendly." What that basically means to you is that they should be free of graphics and fancy formatting. (See Exhibit 2.2.)

Electronic Résumés

Sometimes referred to as plain-text résumés, electronic résumés are designed to be e-mailed to an employer or posted to one of many commercial Internet databases such as CareerMosaic.com, America's Job Bank (ajb.dni.us), or Monster.com.

Some technical considerations:

- Electronic résumés must be written in American Standard Code for Information Interchange (ASCII), which is simply a plain-text format. These characters are universally recognized so that every computer can accurately read and understand them. To create an ASCII file of your current résumé, open your document, then save it as a text or ASCII file. This will eliminate all formatting. Edit as needed using your computer's text editor application.

Exhibit 2.2
DIGITAL RÉSUMÉ

JEFFREY GORDON
Hampton House #480
3400 Michigan Avenue
Los Angeles, CA 90025
Phone: 213-555-4335
E-mail: jgordon@ucla.edu

KEYWORD SUMMARY
B.A. Film, desktop publishing, writing, film history

EDUCATION
B.A. in Film, 2004
UCLA
Los Angeles, CA

WORK EXPERIENCE
Reader, Office Assistant
Atlantic Productions
Santa Monica, CA, 2001-present
* Read and reported on screenplays submitted
for production; performed general office duties;
updated database; scheduled appointments.

Internship
Universal Studios
Orlando, FL 2000-2001
Assistant to the Creative Director
Worked on developing scripts for Nickelodeon
broadcasts.

Publications
Short stories and poems published in a variety of
literary magazines. Sample TV scripts and screenplays
are available upon request.

Put your name at the
top on its own line.

Put your phone number
on its own line.

Keywords make your
résumé easier to find in
a database.

Use a standard-width
typeface.

Use a space between
asterisk and text.

No line should exceed
sixty-five characters.

End each line by
hitting the ENTER
(or RETURN) key.

- Use a standard-width typeface. Courier is a good choice because it is the font associated with ASCII in most systems.
- Use a font size of 11 to 14 points. A 12-point font is considered standard.
- Your margin should be left-justified.
- Do not exceed sixty-five characters per line because the word-wrap function doesn't operate in ASCII.
- Do not use boldface, italics, underlining, bullets, or various font sizes. Instead, use asterisks, plus signs, or all capital letters when you want to emphasize something.
- Avoid graphics and shading.
- Use as many "keywords" as you possibly can. These are words or phrases usually relating to skills or experience that either are specifically used in the job announcement or are popular buzzwords in the industry.
- Minimize abbreviations.
- Your name should be the first line of text.
- Conduct a "test run" by e-mailing your résumé to yourself and a friend before you send it to the employer. See how it transmits, and make any changes you need to. Continue to test it until it's exactly how you want it to look.
- Unless an employer specifically requests that you send the résumé in the form of an attachment, don't. Employers can encounter problems opening a document as an attachment, and there are always viruses to consider.
- Don't forget your cover letter. Send it along with your résumé as a single message.

Scannable Résumés

Some companies are relying on technology to narrow the candidate pool for available job openings. Electronic Applicant Tracking uses imaging to scan, sort, and store résumé elements in a database. Then, through OCR (Optical Character Recognition) software, the computer scans the résumés for keywords and phrases. To have the best chance at getting an interview, you want to increase the number of "hits"—matches of your skills, abilities, experience, and education to those the computer is scanning for—your résumé will get. You can see how critical using the right keywords is for this type of résumé.

Technical considerations include:

- Again, do not use boldface (newer systems may read this OK, but many older ones won't), italics, underlining, bullets, shading, graphics, or multiple font sizes. Instead, for emphasis, use asterisks, plus signs, or all capital letters. Minimize abbreviations.
- Use a popular typeface such as Courier, Helvetica, Ariel, or Palatino. Avoid decorative fonts.
- Font size should be between 11 and 14 points.
- Do not compress the spacing between letters.
- Use horizontal and vertical lines sparingly; the computer may misread them as the letters *L* or *I*.
- Left-justify the text.
- Do not use parentheses or brackets around telephone numbers, and be sure your phone number is on its own line of text.
- Your name should be the first line of text and on its own line. If your résumé is longer than one page, be sure to put your name on the top of all pages.
- Use a traditional résumé structure. The chronological format may work best.
- Use nouns that are skill-focused, such as *management, writer,* and *programming.* This is different from traditional paper résumés, which use action-oriented verbs.
- Laser printers produce the finest copies. Avoid dot-matrix printers.
- Use standard, light-colored paper with text on one side only. Since the higher the contrast, the better, your best choice is black ink on white paper.
- Always send original copies. If you must fax, set the fax on fine mode, not standard.
- Do not staple or fold your résumé. This can confuse the computer.
- Before you send your scannable résumé, be certain the employer uses this technology. If you can't determine this, you may want to send two versions (scannable and traditional) to be sure your résumé gets considered.

Résumé Production and Other Tips

An ink-jet printer is the preferred option for printing your résumé. Begin by printing just a few copies. You may find a small error or you may simply want to make some changes, and it is less frustrating and less expensive if you print in small batches.

Résumé paper color should be carefully chosen. You should consider the types of employers who will receive your résumé and the types of positions for which you are applying. Use white or ivory paper for traditional or conservative employers or for higher-level positions.

Black ink on sharp, white paper can be harsh on the reader's eyes. Think about an ivory or cream paper that will provide less contrast and be easier to read. Pink, green, and blue tints should generally be avoided.

Many résumé writers buy packages of matching envelopes and cover sheet stationery that, although not absolutely necessary, help convey a professional impression.

If you'll be producing many cover letters at home, be sure you have high-quality printing equipment. Learn standard envelope formats for business, and retain a copy of every cover letter you send out. You can use the copies to take notes of any telephone conversations that may occur.

If attending a job fair, either carry a briefcase or place your résumé in a nicely covered legal-size pad holder.

The Cover Letter

The cover letter provides you with the opportunity to tailor your résumé by telling the prospective employer how you can be a benefit to the organization. It allows you to highlight aspects of your background that are not already discussed in your résumé and that might be especially relevant to the organization you are contacting or to the position you are seeking. Every résumé should have a cover letter enclosed when you send it out. Unlike the résumé, which may be mass-produced, a cover letter is most effective when it is individually prepared and focused on the particular requirements of the organization in question.

A good cover letter should supplement the résumé and motivate the reader to review the résumé. The format shown in Exhibit 2.3 (see page 34) is only a suggestion to help you decide what information to include in a cover letter.

Begin the cover letter with your street address six lines down from the top. Leave three to five lines between the date and the name of the person to whom you are addressing the cover letter. Make sure you leave one blank line between the salutation and the body of the letter and between paragraphs. After typing "Sincerely," leave four blank lines and type your name. This should leave plenty of room for your signature. A sample cover letter is shown in Exhibit 2.4 on page 35.

The following guidelines will help you write good cover letters:

1. Be sure to type your letter neatly; ensure there are no misspellings.
2. Avoid unusual typefaces, such as script.
3. Address the letter to an individual, using the person's name and title. To obtain this information, call the company. If answering a blind newspaper advertisement, address the letter "To Whom It May Concern" or omit the salutation.
4. Be sure your cover letter directly indicates the position you are applying for and tells why you are qualified to fill it.
5. Send the original letter, not a photocopy, with your résumé. Keep a copy for your records.
6. Make your cover letter no more than one page.
7. Include a phone number where you can be reached.
8. Avoid trite language and have someone read the letter over to react to its tone, content, and mechanics.
9. For your own information, record the date you send out each letter and résumé.

Exhibit 2.3
COVER LETTER FORMAT

Your Street Address
Your Town, State, Zip
Phone Number
Fax Number
E-mail

Date

Name
Title
Organization
Address

Dear _____:

First Paragraph. In this paragraph state the reason for the letter, name the specific position or type of work you are applying for, and indicate from which resource (career services office, website, newspaper, contact, employment service) you learned of this opening. The first paragraph can also be used to inquire about future openings.

Second Paragraph. Indicate why you are interested in this position, the company, or its products or services and what you can do for the employer. If you are a recent graduate, explain how your academic background makes you a qualified candidate. Try not to repeat the same information found in the résumé.

Third Paragraph. Refer the reader to the enclosed résumé for more detailed information.

Fourth Paragraph. In this paragraph say what you will do to follow up on your letter. For example, state that you will call by a certain date to set up an interview or to find out if the company will be recruiting in your area. Finish by indicating your willingness to answer any questions the recipient may have. Be sure you have provided your phone number.

Sincerely,

Type your name
Enclosure

Exhibit 2.4
SAMPLE COVER LETTER

May 10, 2005

11781 N.W. 11th Street
Miami, FL 33029
E-mail: mkeys@abc.com
Phone: 555-555-6789
Cell: 555-321-4567

Marsha Wells
Director of Human Resources
School Board of Broward County
105 S.E. 2nd Street
Fort Lauderdale, FL 33305

Dear Ms. Wells:

In June 2005, I will graduate from Nova University with a Bachelor of Arts degree in drama education. I read of your opening for an elementary-level drama teacher in the *Fort Lauderdale Sun-Sentinel* on Sunday, May 9, and I am very interested in the possibilities it offers. I am writing to explore the opportunity for employment with your school district.

The ad states that you are looking for a creative person with strong communication skills and leadership ability. I believe that I possess those qualities. During my student teaching assignment at Nova University Day School I learned the importance of teamwork and encouraging students to express their talents.

In addition to the drama and education courses in my academic major program, I have also studied art, music, and psychology. Courses such as music history and child development helped me to understand a wide range of creative influences, and to become familiar with a variety of innovative programs for working with children. I believe that this experience, coupled with my enthusiasm for working in an educational environment, will help me to represent the Broward County School Board in a professional and competent manner.

continued

As you will see on my enclosed résumé, I worked at the Nova Day School and also at a summer camp with a focus on the dramatic arts. I led the camp theater group and helped organize other dramatic presentations. These positions allowed me to gain experience channeling the creative energies of young children through dramatic expression.

I would like the opportunity to meet with you to discuss how my education and experience would be consistent with your needs. I will call your office next week to discuss the possibility of an interview. In the meantime, if you have any questions or require additional information, please contact me at my home, 561-555-2126.

Sincerely,

Melissa Keyes

Enclosure

3

Researching Careers and Networking

"What can I do with my degree?" is a question heard frequently by career counselors. Theater majors have many options, but not all are clearly defined. Although theater majors have narrowed their choices more than some other liberal arts graduates, many still have questions about just how their degree can help them find a career. Unlike students in narrowly defined disciplines such as accounting, computer science, or physical education, theater graduates can face real confusion about just what kinds of jobs they can get with their degrees. While graduates in accounting and computer science usually know what types of jobs they will seek, just what sort of work can theater majors look for?

What Do They Call the Job You Want?

One reason for confusion is perhaps a mistaken assumption that a college education provides job training. In most cases it does not. Of course, applied fields such as engineering, management, or education provide specific skills for the workplace as well as an education. Regardless, your overall college education exposes you to numerous fields of study and teaches you quantitative reasoning, critical thinking, writing, and speaking, all of which can be successfully applied to a number of different job fields. But it still remains up to you to choose a job field and to learn how to articulate the benefits of your education in a way the employer will appreciate.

Collect Job Titles

The world of employment is a complex place, so you need to become a bit of an explorer and adventurer and be willing to try a variety of techniques to develop a list of possible occupations that might use your talents and education. You might find computerized interest inventories, reference books and other sources, and classified ads helpful in this respect. Once you have a list of possibilities that you are interested in and qualified for, you can move on to find out what kinds of organizations have these job titles.

Computerized Interest Inventories. One way to begin collecting job titles is to identify a number of jobs that call for your degree and the particular skills and interests you identified as part of the self-assessment process. There are excellent interactive career-guidance programs on the market to help you produce such selected lists of possible job titles. Most of these are available at colleges and at some larger town and city libraries. Two of the industry leaders are *CHOICES* and *DISCOVER*. Both allow you to enter interests, values, educational background, and other information to produce lists of possible occupations and industries. Each of the resources listed here will produce different job title lists. Some job titles will appear again and again, while others will be unique to a particular source. Investigate all of them!

Reference Sources. Books on the market that may be available through your local library or career counseling office also suggest various occupations related to specific majors. The following are only a few of the many good books on the market: *The College Board Guide to 150 Popular College Majors* and *College Majors and Careers: A Resource Guide for Effective Life Planning* both by Paul Phifer, and *Kaplan's What to Study: 101 Fields in a Flash*. All of these books list possible job titles within the academic major.

The *Occupational Outlook Handbook*, or *OOH*, lists more than two dozen related job titles for theater majors. Some are familiar, such as actor and director. Others are different, such as drama therapist or critic, and indicate the variety of work available within the field.

Occupational Projections and Training Data is another resource that allows you to compare 500 occupations on factors such as job openings, earnings, and training requirements.

These two resources can be used in combination to maximize their value in your job search. For example, if you find stage manager as a job title in the *OOH,* you can look for it in *Occupational Projections and Training Data* and compare it with other jobs related to that title. This will help to add some depth by presenting statistics in a number of different occupations within the same field.

Each job title deserves your consideration. Like removing the layers of an onion, the search for job titles can go on and on! As you spend time doing this activity, you are actually learning more about the value of your degree. What's important in your search at this point is not to become critical or selective but rather to develop as long a list of possibilities as you can. Every source used will help you add new and potentially exciting jobs to your growing list.

Classified Ads. It has been well publicized that the classified ad section of the newspaper represents only a small fraction of the current job market. Nevertheless, the weekly classified ads can be a great help to you in your search. Although they may not be the best place to look for a job, they can teach you a lot about the job market. Classified ads provide a good education in job descriptions, duties, responsibilities, and qualifications. In addition, they provide insight into which industries are actively recruiting and some indication of the area's employment market. This is particularly helpful when seeking a position in a specific geographic area and/or a specific field. For your purposes, classified ads are a good source for job titles to add to your list.

Read the Sunday classified ads in a major market newspaper for several weeks in a row. Cut and paste all the ads that interest you and seem to call for something close to your education, skills, experience, and interests. Remember that classified ads are written for what an organization *hopes* to find; you don't have to meet absolutely every criterion. However, if certain requirements are stated as absolute minimums and you cannot meet them, it's best not to waste your time and that of the employer.

The weekly classified want ads exercise is important because these jobs are out in the marketplace. They truly exist, and people with your qualifications are being sought to apply. What's more, many of these advertisements describe the duties and responsibilities of the job advertised and give you a beginning sense of the challenges and opportunities such a position presents. Some will indicate salary, and that will be helpful as well. This information will better define the jobs for you and provide some good material for possible interviews in that field.

Explore Job Descriptions

Once you've arrived at a solid list of possible job titles that interest you and for which you believe you are somewhat qualified, it's a good idea to do some research on each of these jobs. The preeminent source for such job information is the *Dictionary of Occupational Titles*, or *DOT* (wave.net/upg/ immigration/dot_index.html). This directory lists every conceivable job and provides excellent up-to-date information on duties and responsibilities, interactions with associates, and day-to-day assignments and tasks. These descriptions provide a thorough job analysis, but they do not consider the possible employers or the environments in which a job may be performed. So, although a position as public relations officer may be well defined in terms of duties and responsibilities, it does not explain the differences in doing public relations work in a college or a hospital or a factory or a bank. You will need to look somewhere else for work settings.

Learn More About Possible Work Settings

After reading some job descriptions, you may choose to edit and revise your list of job titles once again, discarding those you feel are not suitable and keeping those that continue to hold your interest. Or you may wish to keep your list intact and see where these jobs may be located. For example, if you are interested in public relations and you appear to have those skills and the requisite education, you'll want to know what organizations do public relations. How can you find that out? How much income does someone in public relations make a year and what is the employment potential for the field of public relations?

To answer these and many other questions about your list of job titles, we recommend you try any of the following resources: *Careers Encyclopedia*, the professional societies and resources found throughout this book, *College to Career: The Guide to Job Opportunities*, and the *Occupational Outlook Handbook* (http://stats.bls.gov/ocohome.htm). Each of these resources, in a different way, will help to put the job titles you have selected into an employer context. Perhaps the most extensive discussion is found in the *Occupational Outlook Handbook*, which gives a thorough presentation of the nature of the work, the working conditions, employment statistics, training, other qualifications, and advancement possibilities as well as job outlook and earnings. Related occupations are also detailed, and a select bibliography is provided to help you find additional information.

Continuing with our public relations example, your search through these reference materials would teach you that the public relations jobs you find attractive are available in larger hospitals, financial institutions, most corporations (both consumer goods and industrial goods), media organizations, and colleges and universities.

Networking

Networking is the process of deliberately establishing relationships to get career-related information or to alert potential employers that you are available for work. Networking is critically important to today's job seeker for two reasons: it will help you get the information you need, and it can help you find out about *all* of the available jobs.

Get the Information You Need

Networkers will review your résumé and give you feedback on its effectiveness. They will talk about the job you are looking for and give you a candid appraisal of how they see your strengths and weaknesses. If they have a good sense of the industry or the employment sector for that job, you'll get their feelings on future trends in the industry as well. Some networkers will be very forthcoming about salaries, job-hunting techniques, and suggestions for your job search strategy. Many have been known to place calls right from the interview desk to friends and associates who might be interested in you. Each networker will make his or her own contribution, and each will be valuable.

Because organizations must evolve to adapt to current global market needs, the information provided by decision makers within various organizations will be critical to your success as a new job market entrant. For example, you might learn about the concept of virtual organizations from a networker. Virtual organizations coordinate economic activity to deliver value to customers by using resources outside the traditional boundaries of the organization. This concept is being discussed and implemented by chief executive officers of many organizations, including Ford Motor, Dell, and IBM. Networking can help you find out about this and other trends currently affecting the industries under your consideration.

Find Out About All of the Available Jobs

Not every job that is available at this very moment is advertised for potential applicants to see. This is called the *hidden job market*. Only 15 to 20 percent of all jobs are formally advertised, which means that 80 to 85 percent of available jobs do not appear in published channels. Networking will help you become more knowledgeable about all the employment opportunities available during your job search period.

Although someone you might talk to today doesn't know of any openings within his or her organization, tomorrow or next week or next month an opening may occur. If you've taken the time to show an interest in and knowledge of their organization, if you've shown the company representative how you can help achieve organizational goals and that you can fit into the organization, you'll be one of the first candidates considered for the position.

Networking: A Proactive Approach

Networking is a proactive rather than a reactive approach. You, as a job seeker, are expected to initiate a certain level of activity on your own behalf; you cannot afford to simply respond to jobs listed in the newspaper. Being proactive means building a network of contacts that includes informed and interested decision makers who will provide you with up-to-date knowledge of the current job market and increase your chances of finding out about employment opportunities appropriate for your interests, experience, and level of education. An old axiom of networking says, "You are only two phone calls away from the information you need." In other words, by talking to enough people, you will quickly come across someone who can offer you help.

Preparing to Network

In deliberately establishing relationships, maximize your efforts by organizing your approach. Five specific areas in which you can organize your efforts include reviewing your self-assessment, reviewing your research on job sites and organizations, deciding who it is you want to talk to, keeping track of all your efforts, and creating your self-promotion tools.

Review Your Self-Assessment

Your self-assessment is as important a tool in preparing to network as it has been in other aspects of your job search. You have carefully evaluated your personal traits, personal values, economic needs, longer-term goals, skill base, preferred skills, and underdeveloped skills. During the networking process you will be called upon to communicate what you know about yourself and relate it to the information or job you seek. Be sure to review the exercises that you completed in the self-assessment section of this book in preparation for networking. We've explained that you need to assess what skills you have acquired from your major that are of general value to an employer and to be ready to express those in ways employers can appreciate as useful in their own organizations.

Review Research on Job Sites and Organizations

In addition, individuals assisting you will expect that you'll have at least some background information on the occupation or industry of interest to you. Refer to the appropriate sections of this book and other relevant publications to acquire the background information necessary for effective networking. They'll explain how to identify not only the job titles that might be of interest to you but also what kinds of organizations employ people to do that job. You will develop some sense of working conditions and expectations about duties and responsibilities—all of which will be of help in your networking interviews.

Decide Who It Is You Want to Talk To

Networking cannot begin until you decide who it is that you want to talk to and, in general, what type of information you hope to gain from your contacts. Once you know this, it's time to begin developing a list of contacts. Five useful sources for locating contacts are described here.

College Alumni Network. Most colleges and universities have created a formal network of alumni and friends of the institution who are particularly interested in helping currently enrolled students and graduates of their alma mater gain employment-related information.

It is usually a simple process to make use of an alumni network. Visit your college's website and locate the alumni office and/or your career center. Either or both sites will have information about your school's alumni network. You'll be provided with information on shadowing experiences, geographic information, or those alumni offering job referrals. If you don't find what you're looking for, don't hesitate to phone or e-mail your career center and ask what they can do to help you connect with an alum.

Alumni networkers may provide some combination of the following services: day-long shadowing experiences, telephone interviews, in-person interviews, information on relocating to given geographic areas, internship information, suggestions on graduate school study, and job vacancy notices.

Present and Former Supervisors. If you believe you are on good terms with present or former job supervisors, they may be an excellent resource for providing information or directing you to appropriate resources that would have information related to your current interests and needs. Additionally, these supervisors probably belong to professional organizations that they might be willing to utilize to get information for you.

Employers in Your Area. Although you may be interested in working in a geographic location different from the one where you currently reside, don't overlook the value of the knowledge and contacts those around you are able to provide. Use the local telephone directory and newspaper to identify the types of organizations you are thinking of working for or professionals who have the kinds of jobs you are interested in. Recently, a call made to a local hospital's financial administrator for information on working in health-care financial administration yielded more pertinent information on training seminars, regional professional organizations, and potential employment sites than a national organization was willing to provide.

Employers in Geographic Areas Where You Hope to Work. If you are thinking about relocating, identifying prospective employers or informational contacts in the new location will be critical to your success. Here are some tips for online searching. First, use a "metasearch" engine to get the most out of your search. Metasearch engines combine several engines into one powerful tool. We frequently use dogpile.com and metasearch.com for this purpose. Try using the city and state as your keywords in a search. *New Haven, Connecticut* will bring you to the city's website with links to the chamber of commerce, member businesses, and other valuable resources. By using looksmart.com you can locate newspapers in any area, and they, too, can provide valuable insight before you relocate. Of course, both dogpile and metasearch can lead you to yellow and white page directories in areas you are considering.

Professional Associations and Organizations. Professional associations and organizations can provide valuable information in several areas: career paths that you might not have considered, qualifications relating to those career choices, publications that list current job openings, and workshops or seminars that will enhance your professional knowledge and skills. They can also be excellent sources for background information on given industries: their health, current problems, and future challenges.

There are several excellent resources available to help you locate professional associations and organizations that would have information to meet your needs. Two especially useful publications are the *Encyclopedia of Associations* and *National Trade and Professional Associations of the United States*.

Keep Track of All Your Efforts

It can be difficult, almost impossible, to remember all the details related to each contact you make during the networking process, so you will want to develop a record-keeping system that works for you. Formalize this process by using your computer to keep a record of the people and organizations you want to contact. You can simply record the contact's name, address, and telephone number, and what information you hope to gain.

You could record this as a simple Word document and you could still use the "Find" function if you were trying to locate some data and could only recall the firm's name or the contact's name. If you're comfortable with database management and you have some database software on your computer, then you can put information at your fingertips even if you have only the zip code! The point here is not technological sophistication but good record keeping.

Once you have created this initial list, it will be helpful to keep more detailed information as you begin to actually make the contacts. Those details should include complete contact information, the date and content of each contact, names and information for additional networkers, and required follow-up. Don't forget to send a letter thanking your contact for his or her time! Your contact will appreciate your recall of details of your meetings and conversations, and the information will help you to focus your networking efforts.

Create Your Self-Promotion Tools

There are two types of promotional tools that are used in the networking process. The first is a résumé and cover letter, and the second is a one-minute "infomercial," which may be given over the telephone or in person.

Techniques for writing an effective résumé and cover letter are discussed in Chapter 2. Once you have reviewed that material and prepared these important documents, you will have created one of your self-promotion tools.

The one-minute infomercial will demand that you begin tying your interests, abilities, and skills to the people or organizations you want to network with. Think about your goal for making the contact to help you understand what you should say about yourself. You should be able to express yourself easily and convincingly. If, for example, you are contacting an alumnus of your institution to obtain the names of possible employment sites in a distant city, be prepared to discuss why you are interested in moving to that location, the types of jobs you are interested in, and the skills and abilities you possess that will make you a qualified candidate.

To create a meaningful one-minute infomercial, write it out, practice it as if it will be a spoken presentation, rewrite it, and practice it again if necessary until expressing yourself comes easily and is convincing.

Here's a simplified example of an infomercial for use over the telephone:

Hello, Mr. Spencer. My name is Susan Reese. I have recently graduated from State College and I am hoping to start a career as a dramatic agent. I have a dual major in theater and business, and believe that I have many skills needed by an agent, such as good interpersonal skills, experience with contract negotiations, and an understanding of the entertainment industry. I also work well under pressure, which I understand can be a real advantage for an agent.

Mr. Spencer, I'm calling you because I still need more information about the agenting business, and I hope that you'll be willing to meet with me for about half an hour to share your views on the profession. I think discussing the different areas of specialization with you might help me to decide which would be best for my skills and experience.

I would be very grateful if you would agree to do this for me. I am available to meet you at your convenience.

It very well may happen that your employer contact wishes you to communicate by e-mail. The infomercial quoted above could easily be rewritten for an e-mail message. You should "cut and paste" your résumé right into the e-mail text itself.

Other effective self-promotion tools include portfolios for those in the arts, writing professions, or teaching. Portfolios show examples of work, photographs of projects or classroom activities, or certificates and credentials that are job related. There may not be an opportunity to use the portfolio during an interview, and it is not something that should be left with the organization. It is designed to be explained and displayed by the creator. However, during some networking meetings, there may be an opportunity to illustrate a point or strengthen a qualification by exhibiting the portfolio.

Beginning the Networking Process

Set the Tone for Your Communications

It can be useful to establish "tone words" for any communications you embark upon. Before making your first telephone call or writing your first letter, decide what you want the person to think of you. If you are networking to try to obtain a job, your tone words might include descriptors such as *genuine*, *informed*, and *self-knowledgeable*. When you're trying to acquire information, your tone words may have a slightly different focus, such as *courteous*, *organized*, *focused*, and *well-spoken*. Use the tone words you establish for your contacts to guide you through the networking process.

Honestly Express Your Intentions

When contacting individuals, it is important to be honest about your reasons for making the contact. Establish your purpose in your own mind and be able and ready to articulate it concisely. Determine an initial agenda, whether it be informational questioning or self-promotion, present it to your contact, and be ready to respond immediately. If you don't adequately prepare before initiating your overture, you may find yourself at a disadvantage if you're asked to immediately begin your informational interview or self-promotion during the first phone conversation or visit.

Start Networking Within Your Circle of Confidence

Once you have organized your approach—by utilizing specific researching methods, creating a system for keeping track of the people you will contact, and developing effective self-promotion tools—you are ready to begin networking. The best way to begin networking is by talking with a group of people you trust and feel comfortable with. This group is usually made up of your family, friends, and career counselors. No matter who is in this inner circle, they will have a special interest in seeing you succeed in your job search. In addition, because they will be easy to talk to, you should try taking some risks in terms of practicing your information-seeking approach. Gain confidence in talking about the strengths you bring to an organization and the underdeveloped skills you feel hinder your candidacy. Be sure to review the section on self-assessment for tips on approaching each of these areas. Ask for critical but constructive feedback from the people in your circle of confidence on the letters you write and the one-minute infomercial you have developed. Evaluate whether you want to make the changes they suggest, then practice the changes on others within this circle.

Stretch the Boundaries of Your Networking Circle of Confidence

Once you have refined the promotional tools you will use to accomplish your networking goals, you will want to make additional contacts. Because you will not know most of these people, it will be a less comfortable activity to undertake. The practice that you gained with your inner circle of trusted friends should have prepared you to now move outside of that comfort zone.

It is said that any information a person needs is only two phone calls away, but the information cannot be gained until you (1) make a reasonable guess about who might have the information you need and (2) pick up the telephone to make the call. Using your network list that includes alumni, instructors, supervisors, employers, and associations, you can begin preparing your list of questions that will allow you to get the information you need.

Prepare the Questions You Want to Ask

Networkers can provide you with the insider's perspective on any given field and you can ask them questions that you might not want to ask in an interview. For example, you can ask them to describe the more repetitious or mundane parts of the job or ask them for a realistic idea of salary expectations. Be sure to prepare your questions ahead of time so that you are organized and efficient.

Be Prepared to Answer Some Questions

To communicate effectively, you must anticipate questions that will be asked of you by the networkers you contact. Revisit the self-assessment process you undertook and the research you've done so that you can effortlessly respond to questions about your short- and long-term goals and the kinds of jobs you are most interested in pursuing.

General Networking Tips

Make Every Contact Count. Setting the tone for each interaction is critical. Approaches that will help you communicate in an effective way include politeness, being appreciative of time provided to you, and being prepared and thorough. Remember, *everyone* within an organization has a circle of influence, so be prepared to interact effectively with each person you encounter in the networking process, including secretarial and support staff. Many information or job seekers have thwarted their own efforts by being rude to some individuals they encountered as they networked because they made the incorrect assumption that certain persons were unimportant.

Sometimes your contacts may be surprised at their ability to help you. After meeting and talking with you, they might think they have not offered much in the way of help. A day or two later, however, they may make a contact that would be useful to you and refer you to that person.

With Each Contact, Widen Your Circle of Networkers. Always leave an informational interview with the names of at least two more people who can help you get the information or job that you are seeking. Don't be shy about asking for additional contacts; networking is all about increasing the number of people you can interact with to achieve your goals.

Make Your Own Decisions. As you talk with different people and get answers to the questions you pose, you may hear conflicting information or get conflicting suggestions. Your job is to listen to these "experts" and decide what information and which suggestions will help you achieve *your* goals. Only implement those suggestions that you believe will work for you.

Shutting Down Your Network

As you achieve the goals that motivated your networking activity—getting the information you need or the job you want—the time will come to inactivate all or parts of your network. As you do, be sure to tell your primary supporters about your change in status. Call or write to each one of them and give them as many details about your new status as you feel is necessary to maintain a positive relationship.

Because a network takes on a life of its own, activity undertaken on your behalf will continue even after you cease your efforts. As you get calls or are contacted in some fashion, be sure to inform these networkers about your change in status, and thank them for assistance they have provided.

Information on the latest employment trends indicates that workers will change jobs or careers several times in their lifetime. Networking, then, will be a critical aspect in the span of your professional life. If you carefully and thoughtfully conduct your networking activities during your job search, you will have a solid foundation of experience when you need to network the next time around.

Where Are These Jobs, Anyway?

Having a list of job titles that you've designed around your own career interests and skills is an excellent beginning. It means you've really thought about who you are and what you are presenting to the employment market. It has caused you to think seriously about the most appealing environments to work in, and you have identified some employer types that represent these environments.

The research and the thinking that you've done thus far will be used again and again. They will be helpful in writing your résumé and cover letters, in talking about yourself on the telephone to prospective employers, and in answering interview questions.

Now is a good time to begin to narrow the field of job titles and employment sites down to some specific employers to initiate the employment contact.

Find Out Which Employers Hire People Like You

This section will provide tips, techniques, and specific resources for developing an actual list of specific employers that can be used to make contacts. It is only an outline that you must be prepared to tailor to your own particular needs and according to what you bring to the job search. Once again, it is important to communicate with others along the way exactly what you're looking for and what your goals are for the research you're doing. Librarians, employers, career counselors, friends, friends of friends, business contacts, and bookstore staff will all have helpful information on geographically specific and new resources to aid you in locating employers who'll hire you.

Identify Information Resources

Your interview wardrobe and your new résumé might have put a dent in your wallet, but the resources you'll need to pursue your job search are available for free. The categories of information detailed here are not hard to find and are yours for the browsing.

Numerous resources described in this section will help you identify actual employers. Use all of them or any others that you identify as available in your geographic area. As you become experienced in this process, you'll quickly figure out which information sources are helpful and which are not. If you live in a rural area, a well-planned day trip to a major city that includes a college career office, a large college or city library, state and federal employment centers, a chamber of commerce office, and a well-stocked bookstore can produce valuable results.

There are many excellent resources available to help you identify actual job sites. They are categorized into employer directories (usually indexed by product lines and geographic location), geographically based directories (designed to highlight particular cities, regions, or states), career-specific directories (e.g., *Sports MarketPlace*, which lists tens of thousands of firms involved with sports), periodicals and newspapers, targeted job posting publications, and videos. This is by no means meant to be a complete treatment of resources but rather a starting point for identifying useful resources.

Working from the more general references to highly specific resources, we provide a basic list to help you begin your search. Many of these you'll find easily available. In some cases reference librarians and others will suggest even better materials for your particular situation. Start to create your own customized bibliography of job search references.

Geographically Based Directories. The Job Bank series published by Bob Adams, Inc. (aip.com) contains detailed entries on each area's major employers, including business activity, address, phone number, and hiring contact name. Many listings specify educational backgrounds being sought in potential employees. Each volume contains a solid discussion of each city's or state's major employment sectors. Organizations are also indexed by industry. Job Bank volumes are available for the following places: Atlanta, Boston, Chicago, Dallas–Ft. Worth, Denver, Detroit, Florida, Houston, Los Angeles, Minneapolis, New York, Ohio, Philadelphia, San Francisco, Seattle, St. Louis, Washington, D.C., and other cities throughout the Northwest.

National Job Bank (careercity.com) lists employers in every state, along with contact names and commonly hired job categories. Included are many small companies often overlooked by other directories. Companies are also indexed by industry. This publication provides information on educational backgrounds sought and lists company benefits.

Periodicals and Newspapers. Several sources are available to help you locate which journals or magazines carry job advertisements in your field. Other resources help you identify opportunities in other parts of the country.

- *Where the Jobs Are: A Comprehensive Directory of 1200 Journals Listing Career Opportunities*
- *Corptech Fast 5000 Company Locator*
- *National Ad Search* (nationaladsearch.com)
- *The Federal Jobs Digest* (jobsfed.com) and *Federal Career Opportunities*
- *World Chamber of Commerce Directory* (chamberofcommerce.org)

This list is certainly not exhaustive; use it to begin your job search work.

Targeted Job Posting Publications. Although the resources that follow are national in scope, they are either targeted to one medium of contact (telephone), focused on specific types of jobs, or less comprehensive than the sources previously listed.

- *Job Hotlines USA* (careers.org/topic/01_002.html)
- *The Job Hunter* (jobhunter.com)
- *Current Jobs for Graduates* (graduatejobs.com)
- *Environmental Opportunities* (ecojobs.com)
- *Y National Vacancy List* (ymcahrm.ns.ca/employed/jobleads.html)
- *ARTSearch*
- *Community Jobs*
- *National Association of Colleges and Employers: Job Choices series*
- *National Association of Colleges and Employers* (naceweb.org)

Videos. You may be one of the many job seekers who likes to get information via a medium other than paper. Many career libraries, public libraries, and career centers in libraries carry an assortment of videos that will help you learn new techniques and get information helpful in the job search.

Locate Information Resources

Throughout these introductory chapters, we have continually referred you to various websites for information on everything from job listings to career information. Using the Web gives you a mobility at your computer that you don't enjoy if you rely solely on books or newspapers or printed journals. Moreover, material on the Web, if the site is maintained, can be the most up-to-date information available.

You'll eventually identify the information resources that work best for you, but make certain you've covered the full range of resources before you begin to rely on a smaller list. Here's a short list of informational sites that many job seekers find helpful:

- Public and college libraries
- College career centers
- Bookstores
- The Internet
- Local and state government personnel offices
- Career/job fairs

Each one of these sites offers a collection of resources that will help you get the information you need.

As you meet and talk with service professionals at all these sites, be sure to let them know what you're doing. Inform them of your job search, what you've already accomplished, and what you're looking for. The more people who know you're job seeking, the greater the possibility that someone will have information or know someone who can help you along your way.

Interviewing and
Job Offer Considerations

Certainly, there can be no one part of the job search process more fraught with anxiety and worry than the interview. Yet seasoned job seekers welcome the interview and will often say, "Just get me an interview and I'm on my way!" They understand that the interview is crucial to the hiring process and equally crucial for them, as job candidates, to have the opportunity of a personal dialogue to add to what the employer may already have learned from the résumé, cover letter, and telephone conversations.

Believe it or not, the interview is to be welcomed, and even enjoyed! It is a perfect opportunity for you, the candidate, to sit down with an employer and express yourself and display who you are and what you want. Of course, it takes thought and planning and a little strategy; after all, it *is* a job interview! But it can be a positive, if not pleasant, experience and one you can look back on and feel confident about your performance and effort.

For many new job seekers, a job, any job, seems a wonderful thing. But seasoned interview veterans know that the job interview is an important step for both sides—the employer and the candidate—to see what each has to offer and whether there is going to be a "fit" of personalities, work styles, and attitudes. And it is this concept of balance in the interview, that both sides have important parts to play, that holds the key to success in mastering this aspect of the job search strategy.

Try to think of the interview as a conversation between two interested and equal partners. You both have important, even vital, information to deliver and to learn. Of course, there's no denying the employer has some leverage, especially in the initial interview for recruitment or any interview scheduled by the candidate and not the recruiter. That should not prevent the interviewee from seeking to play an equal part in what should be a fair exchange of information. Too often the untutored candidate allows the interview to become one-sided. The employer asks all the questions and the candidate simply responds. The ideal would be for two mutually interested parties to sit down and discuss possibilities for each. This is a conversation of significance, and it requires preparation, thought about the tone of the interview, and planning of the nature and details of the information to be exchanged.

Preparing for the Interview

The length of most initial interviews is about thirty minutes. Given the brevity, the information that is exchanged ought to be important. The candidate should be delivering material that the employer cannot discover on the résumé, and in turn, the candidate should be learning things about the employer that he or she could not otherwise find out. After all, if you have only thirty minutes, why waste time on information that is already published? The information exchanged is more than just factual, and both sides will learn much from what they see of each other, as well. How the candidate looks, speaks, and acts are important to the employer. The employer's attention to the interview and awareness of the candidate's résumé, the setting, and the quality of information presented are important to the candidate.

Just as the employer has every right to be disappointed when a prospect is late for the interview, looks unkempt, and seems ill-prepared to answer fairly standard questions, the candidate may be disappointed with an interviewer who isn't ready for the meeting, hasn't learned the basic résumé facts, and is constantly interrupted by telephone calls. In either situation there's good reason to feel let down.

There are many elements to a successful interview, and some of them are not easy to describe or prepare for. Sometimes there is just a chemistry between interviewer and interviewee that brings out the best in both, and a good exchange takes place. But there is much the candidate can do to pave the way for success in terms of his or her résumé, personal appearance, goals, and interview strategy—each of which we will discuss. However, none of this preparation is as important as the time and thought the candidate gives to personal self-assessment.

Self-Assessment
Neither a stunning résumé nor an expensive, well-tailored suit can compensate for candidates who do not know what they want, where they are going,

or why they are interviewing with a particular employer. Self-assessment, the process by which we begin to know and acknowledge our own particular blend of education, experiences, needs, and goals, is not something that can be sorted out the weekend before a major interview. Of all the elements of interview preparation, this one requires the longest lead time and cannot be faked.

Because the time allotted for most interviews is brief, it is all the more important for job candidates to understand and express succinctly why they are there and what they have to offer. This is not a time for undue modesty (or for braggadocio either); it is a time for a compelling, reasoned statement of why you feel that you and this employer might make a good match. It means you have to have thought about your skills, interests, and attributes; related those to your life experiences and your own history of challenges and opportunities; and determined what that indicates about your strengths, preferences, values, and areas needing further development.

If you need some assistance with self-assessment issues, refer to Chapter 1. Included are suggested exercises that can be done as needed, such as making up an experiential diary and extracting obvious strengths and weaknesses from past experiences. These simple assignments will help you look at past activities as collections of tasks with accompanying skills and responsibilities. Don't overlook your high school or college career office. Many offer personal counseling on self-assessment issues and may provide testing instruments such as the *Myers-Briggs Type Indicator (MBTI)*, the *Harrington-O'Shea Career Decision-Making System (CDM)*, the *Strong Interest Inventory (SII)*, or any other of a wide selection of assessment tools that can help you clarify some of these issues prior to the interview stage of your job search.

The Résumé

Résumé preparation has been discussed in detail, and some basic examples were provided. In this section we want to concentrate on how best to use your résumé in the interview. In most cases the employer will have seen the résumé prior to the interview, and, in fact, it may well have been the quality of that résumé that secured the interview opportunity.

An interview is a conversation, however, and not an exercise in reading. So, if the employer hasn't seen your résumé and you have brought it along to the interview, wait until asked or until the end of the interview to offer it. Otherwise, you may find yourself staring at the back of your résumé and simply answering "yes" and "no" to a series of questions drawn from that document.

Sometimes an interviewer is not prepared and does not know or recall the contents of the résumé and may use the résumé to a greater or lesser degree as a "prompt" during the interview. It is for you to judge what that may indicate about the individual performing the interview or the employer. If your interviewer seems surprised by the scheduled meeting, relies on the résumé to an inordinate degree, and seems otherwise unfamiliar with your background, this lack of preparation for the hiring process could well be a symptom of general management disorganization or may simply be the result of poor planning on the part of one individual. It is your responsibility as a potential employee to be aware of these signals and make your decisions accordingly.

In any event, it is perfectly acceptable for you to get the conversation back to a more interpersonal style by saying something like, "Mr. Smith, you might be interested in some recent experience I gained in an internship that is not detailed on my résumé. May I tell you about it?" This can return the interview to two people talking to each other, not one reading and the other responding.

By all means, bring at least one copy of your résumé to the interview. Occasionally, at the close of an interview, an interviewer will express an interest in circulating a résumé to several departments, and you could then offer the copy you brought. Sometimes, an interview appointment provides an opportunity to meet others in the organization who may express an interest in you and your background, and it may be helpful to follow up with a copy of your résumé. Our best advice, however, is to keep it out of sight until needed or requested.

Employer Information

Whether your interview is for graduate school admission, an overseas corporate position, or a position with a local company, it is important to know something about the employer or the organization. Keeping in mind that the interview is relatively brief and that you will hopefully have other interviews with other organizations, it is important to keep your research in proportion. If secondary interviews are called for, you will have additional time to do further research. For the first interview, it is helpful to know the organization's mission, goals, size, scope of operations, and so forth. Your research may uncover recent areas of challenge or particular successes that may help to fuel the interview. Use the "What Do They Call the Job You Want?" section of Chapter 3, your library, and your career or guidance office to help you locate this information in the most efficient way possible. Don't be shy in asking advice of these counseling and guidance professionals on how best to spend your preparation time. With some practice, you'll soon learn how much information is enough and which kinds of information are most useful to you.

Interview Content

We've already discussed how it can help to think of the interview as an important conversation—one that, as with any conversation, you want to find pleasant and interesting and to leave you with a good feeling. But because this conversation is especially important, the information that's exchanged is critical to its success. What do you want them to know about you? What do you need to know about them? What interview technique do you need to particularly pay attention to? How do you want to manage the close of the interview? What steps will follow in the hiring process?

Except for the professional interviewer, most of us find interviewing stressful and anxiety-provoking. Developing a strategy before you begin interviewing will help you relieve some stress and anxiety. One particular strategy that has worked for many and may work for you is interviewing by objective. Before you interview, write down three to five goals you would like to achieve for that interview. They may be technique goals: smile a little more, have a firmer handshake, be sure to ask about the next stage in the interview process before leaving. They may be content-oriented goals: find out about the company's current challenges and opportunities; be sure to speak of your recent research, writing experiences, or foreign travel. Whatever your goals, jot down a few of them as goals for each interview.

Most people find that in trying to achieve these few goals, their interviewing technique becomes more organized and focused. After the interview, the most common question friends and family ask is "How did it go?" With this technique, you have an indication of whether you met *your* goals for the meeting, not just some vague idea of how it went. Chances are, if you accomplished what you wanted to, it improved the quality of the entire interview. As you continue to interview, you will want to revise your goals to continue improving your interview skills.

Now, add to the concept of the significant conversation the idea of a beginning, a middle, and a closing and you will have two thoughts that will give your interview a distinctive character. Be sure to make your introduction warm and cordial. Say your full name (and if it's a difficult-to-pronounce name, help the interviewer to pronounce it) and make certain you know your interviewer's name and how to pronounce it. Most interviews begin with some "soft talk" about the weather, chat about the candidate's trip to the interview site, or national events. This is done as a courtesy to relax both you and the interviewer, to get you talking, and to generally try to defuse the atmosphere of excessive tension. Try to be yourself, engage in the conversation, and don't try to second-guess the interviewer. This is simply what it appears to be—casual conversation.

Once you and the interviewer move on to exchange more serious information in the middle part of the interview, the two most important concerns become your ability to handle challenging questions and your success at asking meaningful ones. Interviewer questions will probably fall into one of three categories: personal assessment and career direction, academic assessment, and knowledge of the employer. Here are a few examples of questions in each category:

Personal Assessment and Career Direction
1. What motivates you to put forth your best effort?
2. What do you consider to be your greatest strengths and weaknesses?
3. What qualifications do you have that make you think you will be successful in this career?

Academic Assessment
1. What led you to choose your major?
2. What subjects did you like best and least? Why?
3. How has your college experience prepared you for this career?

Knowledge of the Employer
1. What do you think it takes to be successful in an organization like ours?
2. In what ways do you think you can make a contribution to our organization?
3. Why did you choose to seek a position with this organization?

The interviewer wants a response to each question but is also gauging your enthusiasm, preparedness, and willingness to communicate. In each response you should provide some information about yourself that can be related to the employer's needs. A common mistake is to give too much information. Answer each question completely, but be careful not to run on too long with extensive details or examples.

Questions About Underdeveloped Skills

Most employers interview people who have met some minimum criteria of education and experience. They interview candidates to see who they are, to learn what kind of personality they exhibit, and to get some sense of how they might fit into the existing organization. It may be that you are asked about skills the employer hopes to find and that you have not documented. Maybe it's grant-writing experience, knowledge of the European political system, or a knowledge of the film world.

To questions about skills and experiences you don't have, answer honestly and forthrightly and try to offer some additional information about skills you do have. For example, perhaps the employer is disappointed you have no grant-writing experience. An honest answer may be as follows:

No, unfortunately, I was never in a position to acquire those skills. I do understand something of the complexities of the grant-writing process and feel confident that my attention to detail, careful reading skills, and strong writing would make grants a wonderful challenge in a new job. I think I could get up on the learning curve quickly.

The employer hears an honest admission of lack of experience but is reassured by some specific skill details that do relate to grant writing and a confident manner that suggests enthusiasm and interest in a challenge.

For many students, questions about their possible contribution to an employer's organization can prove challenging. Because your education has probably not included specific training for a job, you need to review your academic record and select capabilities you have developed in your major that an employer can appreciate. For example, perhaps you read well and can analyze and condense what you've read into smaller, more focused pieces. That could be valuable. Or maybe you did some serious research and you know you have valuable investigative skills. Your public speaking might be highly developed and you might use visual aids appropriately and effectively. Or maybe your skill at correspondence, memos, and messages is effective. Whatever it is, you must take it out of the academic context and put it into a new, employer-friendly context so your interviewer can best judge how you could help the organization.

Exhibiting knowledge of the organization will, without a doubt, show the interviewer that you are interested enough in the available position to have done some legwork in preparation for the interview. Remember, it is not necessary to know every detail of the organization's history but rather to have a general knowledge about why it is in business and how the industry is faring.

Sometime during the interview, generally after the midway point, you'll be asked if you have any questions for the interviewer. Your questions will tell the employer much about your attitude and your desire to understand the organization's expectations so you can compare them to your own strengths. The following are just a few questions you might want to ask:

1. What is the communication style of the organization? (meetings, memos, and so forth)
2. What would a typical day in this position be like for me?
3. What have been some of the interesting challenges and opportunities your organization has recently faced?

Most interviews draw to a natural closing point, so be careful not to prolong the discussion. At a signal from the interviewer, wind up your presentation, express your appreciation for the opportunity, and be sure to ask what the next stage in the process will be. When can you expect to hear from them? Will they be conducting second-tier interviews? If you are interested and haven't heard, would they mind a phone call? Be sure to collect a business card with the name and phone number of your interviewer. On your way out, you might have an opportunity to pick up organizational literature you haven't seen before.

With the right preparation—a thorough self-assessment, professional clothing, and employer information—you'll be able to set and achieve the goals you have established for the interview process.

Interview Follow-Up

Quite often there is a considerable time lag between interviewing for a position and being hired or, in the case of the networker, between your phone call or letter to a possible contact and the opportunity of a meeting. This can be frustrating. "Why aren't they contacting me?" "I thought I'd get another interview, but no one has telephoned." "Am I out of the running?" You don't know what is happening.

Consider the Differing Perspectives

Of course, there is another perspective—that of the networker or hiring organization. Organizations are complex, with multiple tasks that need to be accomplished each day. Hiring is a discrete activity that does not occur as frequently as other job assignments. The hiring process might have to take second place to other, more immediate organizational needs. Although it may be very important to you, and it is certainly ultimately significant to the employer, other issues such as fiscal management, planning and product development, employer vacation periods, or financial constraints may prevent an organization or individual within that organization from acting on your employment or your request for information as quickly as you or they would prefer.

Use Your Communication Skills

Good communication is essential here to resolve any anxieties, and the responsibility is on you, the job or information seeker. Too many job seekers and networkers offer as an excuse that they don't want to "bother" the organization by writing letters or calling. Let us assure you here and now, once and for all, that if you are troubling an organization by over-communicating, someone will indicate that situation to you quite clearly. If not, you can only assume you are a worthwhile prospect and the employer appreciates being reminded of your availability and interest. Let's look at follow-up practices in the job interview process and the networking situation separately.

Following Up on the Employment Interview

A brief thank-you note following an interview is an excellent and polite way to begin a series of follow-up communications with a potential employer with whom you have interviewed and want to remain in touch. It should be just that—a thank-you for a good meeting. If you failed to mention some fact or experience during your interview that you think might add to your candidacy, you may use this note to do that. However, this should be essentially a note whose overall tone is appreciative and, if appropriate, indicative of a continuing interest in pursuing any opportunity that may exist with that organization. It is one of the few pieces of business correspondence that may be handwritten, but always use plain, good-quality, standard-size paper.

If, however, at this point you are no longer interested in the employer, the thank-you note is an appropriate time to indicate that. You are under no obligation to identify any reason for not continuing to pursue employment with that organization, but if you are so inclined to indicate your professional reasons (pursuing other employers more akin to your interests, looking for greater income production than this employer can provide, a different geographic location), you certainly may. It should not be written with an eye to negotiation, for it will not be interpreted as such.

As part of your interview closing, you should have taken the initiative to establish lines of communication for continuing information about your candidacy. If you asked permission to telephone, wait a week following your thank-you note, then telephone your contact simply to inquire how things are progressing on your employment status. The feedback you receive here should be taken at face value. If your interviewer simply has no information, he or she will tell you so and indicate whether you should call again and when. Don't be discouraged if this should continue over some period of time.

If during this time something occurs that you think improves or changes your candidacy (some new qualification or experience you may have had), including any offers from other organizations, by all means telephone or write to inform the employer about this. In the case of an offer from a competing but less desirable or equally desirable organization, telephone your contact, explain what has happened, express your real interest in the organization, and inquire whether some determination on your employment might be made before you must respond to this other offer. An organization that is truly interested in you may be moved to make a decision about your candidacy. Equally possible is the scenario in which they are not yet ready to make a decision and so advise you to take the offer that has been presented. Again, you have no ethical alternative but to deal with the information presented in a straightforward manner.

When accepting other employment, be sure to contact any employers still actively considering you and inform them of your new job. Thank them graciously for their consideration. There are many other job seekers out there just like you who will benefit from having their candidacy improved when others bow out of the race. Who knows, you might at some future time have occasion to interact professionally with one of the organizations with which you sought employment. How embarrassing it would be to have someone remember you as the candidate who failed to notify them that you were taking a job elsewhere!

In all of your follow-up communications, keep good notes of whom you spoke with, when you called, and any instructions that were given about return communications. This will prevent any misunderstandings and provide you with good records of what has transpired.

Job Offer Considerations

For many recent college graduates, the thrill of their first job and, for some, the most substantial regular income they have ever earned seems an excess of good fortune coming at once. To question that first income or to be critical in any way of the conditions of employment at the time of the initial offer seems like looking a gift horse in the mouth. It doesn't seem to occur to many new hires even to attempt to negotiate any aspect of their first job. And, as many employers who deal with entry-level jobs for recent college graduates will readily confirm, the reality is that there simply isn't much movement in salary available to these new college recruits. The entry-level hire generally does not have an employment track record on a professional level to provide any leverage for negotiation. Real negotiations on salary, benefits, retirement provisions, and so forth come to those with significant employment records at higher income levels.

Of course, the job offer is more than just money. It can be composed of geographic assignment, duties and responsibilities, training, benefits, health and medical insurance, educational assistance, car allowance or company vehicle, and a host of other items. All of this is generally detailed in the formal letter that presents the final job offer. In most cases this is a follow-up to a personal phone call from the employer representative who has been principally responsible for your hiring process.

That initial telephone offer is certainly binding as a verbal agreement, but most firms follow up with a detailed letter outlining the most significant parts of your employment contract. You may, of course, choose to respond immediately at the time of the telephone offer (which would be considered a binding oral contract), but you will also be required to formally answer the letter of offer with a letter of acceptance, restating the salient elements of the employer's description of your position, salary, and benefits. This ensures that both parties are clear on the terms and conditions of employment and remuneration and any other outstanding aspects of the job offer.

Is This the Job You Want?

Most new employees will respond affirmatively in writing, glad to be in the position to accept employment. If you've worked hard to get the offer and the job market is tight, other offers may not be in sight, so you will say, "Yes, I accept!" What is important here is that the job offer you accept be one that does fit your particular needs, values, and interests as you've outlined them in your self-assessment process. Moreover, it should be a job that will not only use your skills and education but also challenge you to develop new skills and talents.

Jobs are sometimes accepted too hastily, for the wrong reasons, and without proper scrutiny by the applicant. For example, an individual might readily accept a sales job only to find the continual rejection by potential clients unendurable. An office worker might realize within weeks the constraints of a desk job and yearn for more activity. Employment is an important part of our lives. It is, for most of our adult lives, our most continuous productive activity. We want to make good choices based on the right criteria.

If you have a low tolerance for risk, a job based on commission will certainly be very anxiety-provoking. If being near your family is important, issues of relocation could present a decision crisis for you. If you're an adventurous person, a job with frequent travel would provide needed excitement and be very desirable. The importance of income, the need to continue your education, your personal health situation—all of these have an impact on whether the job you are considering will ultimately meet your needs. Unless you've spent some time understanding and thinking about these issues, it will be difficult to evaluate offers you do receive.

More important, if you make a decision that you cannot tolerate and feel you must leave that job, you will then have both unemployment and self-esteem issues to contend with. These will combine to make the next job search tough going, indeed. So make your acceptance a carefully considered decision.

Negotiate Your Offer

It may be that there is some aspect of your job offer that is not particularly attractive to you. Perhaps there is no relocation allotment to help you move your possessions, and this presents some financial hardship for you. It may be that the health insurance is less than you had hoped. Your initial assignment may be different from what you expected, either in its location or in the duties and responsibilities that comprise it. Or it may simply be that the salary is less than you anticipated. Other considerations may be your official starting date of employment, vacation time, evening hours, dates of training programs or schools, and other concerns.

If you are considering not accepting the job because of some item or items in the job offer "package" that do not meet your needs, you should know that most employers emphatically wish that you would bring that issue to their attention. It may be that the employer can alter it to make the offer more agreeable for you. In some cases it cannot be changed. In any event the employer would generally like to have the opportunity to try to remedy a difficulty rather than risk losing a good potential employee over an issue that might have been resolved. After all, they have spent time and funds in securing your services, and they certainly deserve an opportunity to resolve any possible differences.

Honesty is the best approach in discussing any objections or uneasiness you might have over the employer's offer. Having received your formal offer in writing, contact your employer representative and indicate your particular dissatisfaction in a straightforward manner. For example, you might explain that while you are very interested in being employed by this organization, the salary (or any other benefit) is less than you have determined you require. State the terms you need, and listen to the response. You may be asked to put this in writing, or you may be asked to hold off until the firm can decide on a response. If you are dealing with a senior representative of the organization, one who has been involved in hiring for some time, you may get an immediate response or a solid indication of possible outcomes.

Perhaps the issue is one of relocation. Your initial assignment is in the Midwest, and because you had indicated a strong West Coast preference, you are surprised at the actual assignment. You might simply indicate that while you understand the need for the company to assign you based on its needs, you are disappointed and had hoped to be placed on the West Coast. You could inquire if that were still possible and, if not, would it be reasonable to expect a West Coast relocation in the future.

If your request is presented in a reasonable way, most employers will not see this as jeopardizing your offer. If they can agree to your proposal, they will. If not, they will simply tell you so, and you may choose to continue your candidacy with them or remove yourself from consideration. The choice will be up to you.

Some firms will adjust benefits within their parameters to meet the candidate's need if at all possible. If a candidate requires a relocation cost allowance, he or she may be asked to forgo tuition benefits for the first year to accomplish this adjustment. An increase in life insurance may be adjusted by some other benefit trade-off; perhaps a family dental plan is not needed. In these decisions you are called upon, sometimes under time pressure, to know how you value these issues and how important each is to you.

Many employers find they are more comfortable negotiating for candidates who have unique qualifications or who bring especially needed expertise to the organization. Employers hiring large numbers of entry-level college graduates may be far more reluctant to accommodate any changes in offer conditions. They are well supplied with candidates with similar education and experience so that if rejected by one candidate, they can draw new candidates from an ample labor pool.

Compare Offers

The condition of the economy, the job seeker's academic major and particular geographic job market, and individual needs and demands for certain employment conditions may not provide more than one job offer at a time. Some job seekers may feel that no reasonable offer should go unaccepted for the simple fear there won't be another.

In a tough job market, or if the job you seek is not widely available, or when your job search goes on too long and becomes difficult to sustain financially and emotionally, it may be necessary to accept an inferior offer. The alternative is continued unemployment. Even here, when you feel you don't have a choice, you can at least understand that in accepting this particular offer, there may be limitations and conditions you don't appreciate. At the time of acceptance, there were no other alternatives, but you can begin to use that position to gain the experience and talent to move toward a more attractive position.

Sometimes, however, more than one offer is received, and the candidate has the luxury of choice. If the job seeker knows what he or she wants and has done the necessary self-assessment honestly and thoroughly, it may be clear that one of the offers conforms more closely to those expressed wants and needs.

However, if, as so often happens, the offers are similar in terms of conditions and salary, the question then becomes which organization might provide the necessary climate, opportunities, and advantages for your professional development and growth. This is the time when solid employer research and astute questioning during the interviews really pay off. How much did you learn about the employer through your own research and skillful questioning? When the interviewer asked during the interview "Do you have any questions?" did you ask the kinds of questions that would help resolve a choice between one organization and another? Just as an employer must decide among numerous applicants, so must the applicant learn to assess the potential employer. Both are partners in the job search.

Reneging on an Offer

An especially disturbing occurrence for employers and career counseling professionals is when a job seeker formally (either orally or by written contract) accepts employment with one organization and later reneges on the agreement and goes with another employer.

There are all kinds of rationalizations offered for this unethical behavior. None of them satisfies. The sad irony is that what the job seeker is willing to do to the employer—make a promise and then break it—he or she would be outraged to have done to him- or herself: have the job offer pulled. It is a very bad way to begin a career. It suggests the individual has not taken the time to do the necessary self-assessment and self-awareness exercises to think and judge critically. The new offer taken may, in fact, be no better or worse than the one refused. You should be aware that there have been incidents of legal action following job candidates' reneging on an offer. This adds a very sour note to what should be a harmonious beginning of a lifelong adventure.

PART TWO

THE CAREER PATHS

Introduction to the Theater Career Paths

"In all ages the drama . . . through its portrayal of the acting and suffering spirit of man, has been more closely allied than any other art to his deeper thoughts concerning his nature and destiny."
—LUDWIG LEWISOHN

How can you best express your love for theater through a profitable career? You must examine your skills, abilities, strengths, weaknesses, priorities, goals, dreams, and hopes to determine which aspect of the world of theater is most appealing and most possible for you. Then ask yourself the following questions: Which aspects of the world of theater do I enjoy most? Am I more attracted to the stage, television, radio, movies, or commercials? Do I want a nine-to-five job? Do I mind traveling? Do I enjoy being the center of attention?

Would I prefer to work behind the scenes? Am I creative? Do I like working in a group situation? Do I mind working long hours? Do I like the idea of being my own boss? Am I good at passing along information to others? Do I like to be in charge? Would I prefer to have others in charge? Do I enjoy working with adults or children? Would I prefer doing a variety of things—or only one? Do I prefer to work primarily with my hands or my mind?

Your answers to these questions will be a starting point for considering your job options as a theater major.

In This Book

This book does not provide information about every possible career for a theater major. The chapters that follow offer an abundance of information about many careers in this field and they all have one element in common: all provide you with the opportunity to express your love for the world of theater.

The five career paths described in this book include:

1. Performing
2. Behind the Scenes
3. The Business of Theater
4. Teaching Theater
5. Other Theater Careers

Theater is a very wide field that provides many opportunities for those who are willing to prepare themselves and work hard to achieve success. Read on to determine which area of theater appeals to you most, and then take the necessary steps to fulfill your dreams.

6

Path I: Performing

*"Simply what cannot be expressed by any other means. . . .
A complexity of words, movements, gestures that convey a
vision of the world unexpressible in any other way."*
—EUGENE IONESCO

Many people, particularly those who are young, dream of becoming famous actors or actresses. Though only a small percentage succeed, a large number try. Is performing in theater your dream?

Achieving success requires a combination of education, talent, hard work, experience, and luck—not necessarily in that order. Do you think you have what it takes to become one of the estimated 150,000 actors and actresses who are actively performing in the United States today?

Definition of the Career Path

Actors and actresses are performers who play roles or parts in comedic, musical, or dramatic productions. This includes performances in stage, television, video, radio, and motion picture productions. In an attempt to both communicate and entertain, actors use speech, gestures, movement, and body language. In this way they operate as the principals who tell us a story.

The work of actors begins long before they perform in front of an audience or camera. Prior to the actual production, they analyze the theme of the play, study the script, scrutinize the character they are to play, memorize the lines, gain a concrete understanding of the director's viewpoint, become familiar with the cues that bring them on and off stage, and often spend long, tedious hours in rehearsals.

In some ways, the medium in which actors work (whether on the stage, in movies, or in television) determines to what extent they must prepare for

CASTING NOTICE: OPEN AUDITION—TOWN PLAYHOUSE

Town Playhouse will hold open auditions for its new season. Auditions will be held in Florida, Saturday, March 25, from 11 A.M. to 4 P.M. at the Town Playhouse, 1234 Barclay Drive, Braver, Florida, and in New York, the first week of April. Performers should prepare two contrasting monologues, not to exceed four minutes combined. Those who are auditioning will be seen in the order of their arrival. The current schedule includes Shakespeare's *The Comedy of Errors*, rehearsals to begin May 25; *Camping with Henry and Tom*, rehearsals to begin August 2; *Bell, Book and Candle*, rehearsals to begin September 30; and *To Kill a Mockingbird*, rehearsals to begin November 10. Rehearsals will last for three-and-a-half weeks. Contracts will run for two to seven months. Every position is paid, and all roles are open. No calls please.

their parts. For example, performers assigned roles in musical comedies played on stage may not only have to memorize speaking lines but also sing, dance, and carry out other functions in connection with their parts. (This may mean taking vocal or dancing instructions to fulfill the requirements of the role.) Their roles may require them to speak with appropriate accents or speech patterns associated with the characters or the locale of the production (such as in *West Side Story*) or to learn distinctive physical movements and gestures that are specific to the characters they are playing (as in *The Lion King*). In some cases, they may be required to apply appropriate makeup, although in many cases, makeup artists are employed to accomplish this.

Actors and actresses who perform in stage shows generally rehearse for longer periods of time than do radio or television performers. Lines, actions, and cues must be perfect before the public sees the show. Musicals and stage plays may run for weeks or even years, although the people assuming the various roles may change. Rehearsals for a drama production may run about four weeks, while musicals may take one or two additional weeks.

Radio performers are not required to practice as extensively as stage or film performers must because they can read their lines without having to memorize them. However, they must be able to express a lot of feeling and emotion with their voices so that listeners may gain an understanding and appreciation for the characters without ever seeing them.

Weekly television shows and commercials are frequently filmed or taped in shorter periods of time. Miniseries or specials may call for longer periods

CASTING NOTICE: BRAVO PLAYERS

Auditions will be held for the upcoming season of the Bravo Players on Tuesday, July 19, from 4:00 P.M. until 8:00 P.M. at the Bravo Players Theater, 436 Broadway, New York. The season runs from September through May with 35 consistent, full-paid weeks. Performances will be mostly in the metropolitan area with a few overnights and a total of ten weeks in New York City. Audition material will be provided. Salary is approximately $600 per week.

of rehearsal time. Many of the television programs currently being scheduled are weekly series, and all rehearsals and filming are accomplished in six days or less. Special shows or films made exclusively for television take much more preparation than weekly series shows. Because most television productions are prerecorded on film or videotape, the rehearsal and filming techniques are similar to those used by the movie industry.

Generally, movie actors and actresses don't rehearse a movie from the beginning to the end. They work on small segments one at a time, and the cameras roll to film these short scenes. Later, the film editors put the scenes in proper order.

Only a few actors ever achieve recognition as stars in stage, television, or motion pictures. A larger number of well-known, experienced performers are frequently cast in supporting roles. Others work as "extras," with no lines to deliver, or make brief cameo appearances, speaking only one or two lines. Sometimes, hundreds of extras are hired for movies—especially for the filming of large-scale events, such as the Super Bowl. To work as a movie extra, an actor must usually be listed by a casting agency, such as Central Casting, a no-fee agency that supplies all extras to the major movie studios in Hollywood. Applicants are accepted only when the number of persons of a particular type on the list—for example, athletic young women, old men, or small children—is below the foreseeable need.

Between engagements, actors refine and develop their talents by taking vocal, dancing, and acting lessons. Some do voice-over and narration work for advertisements, animated features, books on tape, and other electronic media. They may also teach in high school or university drama departments, acting conservatories, or public programs.

Many actors also make personal appearances and accept offers to perform at benefit shows.

Possible Job Titles

Actor
Actress
Comic actor or actress
Day performer
Dramatic artist
Extra
Ingenue
Leading man or woman
Live theater performer
Motion picture artist
Movie star
Musical comedy star
Performer
Performer of commercials
Radio performer
Screen actor
Screen performer
Stage actor
Stage performer
Television actor
Voice-over artist

Possible Employers

Performers are hired for stage shows, for appearances in film, for commercials, and for parts on radio and television. New York and Hollywood are the most likely places to acquire employment. Next most likely would be Boston, Chicago, Seattle, Dallas, Miami, Minneapolis, San Francisco,

CASTING NOTICE: *DRIVING MISS DAISY*—WISCONSIN

Submissions are now being accepted for *Driving Miss Daisy*, which will be performed in Wisconsin with the Stonehouse Playhouse in Sycamore. Rehearsals will take place in August and performances will be given in September. Salary and housing provided. Please fax your résumé to (414) 656-7777.

CASTING NOTICE: PROFESSIONAL TOURING COMPANY SEEKS PERFORMERS

Barclay Productions is preparing for their fall and spring touring season. Productions include *Beauty and the Beast, Rumpelstiltskin, Cinderella, The Silly Adventures of Sinbad, Hercules,* and *Snow White and the Seven Dwarfs.* Performers must also be able to sing and move well. We are especially interested in a group of actors to fill the following: ingenues, young leading men and women, and comic actors. Consideration will be given for the fall-spring season, touring the Tri-State Area. All actors will be paid. If you have previously sent a photo/resume, just send a postcard to: Barclay Productions, 168 Elm Street, Edison, New Jersey.

Toronto, and Vancouver. However, most large cities have some kind of theater groups. And even smaller towns usually have acting groups that offer a chance to gain some experience and employment. These would include little theaters, children's theaters, and regional and community theaters. Summer stock tours take actors and actresses all around the United States and Canada.

Related Occupations

People who work in occupations requiring acting skills include dancers, choreographers, disc jockeys, comedians, impersonators, mimes, puppeteers, ventriloquists, magicians, clowns, drama teachers or coaches, and radio and television announcers. Others working in occupations related to acting are playwrights, scriptwriters, stage managers, costume designers, makeup art-

CASTING NOTICE: PETRE PLAYERS PLAYHOUSE

Petre Players Playhouse will hold open auditions for its fall season. Auditions will be held in Chicago on Saturday, September 1, beginning at 10:00 A.M. and at the Petre Playhouse in New York the first week of September. Performers should prepare a four-minute monologue. Those who audition will be seen in order of their arrival. All positions are paid and all roles are open. Plays will include *The Miser* and *The Business of Murder.*

ists, hair stylists, lighting designers, and set designers. Workers in occupations involved with the business aspects of theater productions include managing directors; company managers; booking managers; publicists; and agents for actors, directors, or playwrights.

Working Conditions

Most actors work under pressure, faced with the anxiety of unsteady employment and the possibility of negative reviews and rejection. Many face stress from the continual need to find their next job. To succeed, actors need patience and commitment to their craft.

Actors strive to deliver flawless performances, often while working under undesirable and unpleasant conditions. Performers must be available for constant rehearsals, which may be both physically and mentally stressful and exhausting. Actors often spend several weeks rehearsing their parts, and some rehearsals are scheduled on weekends, holidays, and evenings. Those having small roles may wait for hours before being called to rehearse their parts.

Rehearsals may take place amid the clutter of electricians, camera operators, painters, carpenters, and stagehands. Heavy costumes and hot lights may be necessary. Deadlines loom in this business too—and performers may be called upon to accomplish quite a bit in a very short period of time. In fact, a performer may rehearse one production in the morning and afternoon and perform another every evening.

When performing, actors typically work long, irregular hours. For example, stage actors may perform one show at night while rehearsing another during the day. They also might travel with a show when it tours the country. Movie actors may work on location, sometimes under adverse weather conditions, and may spend considerable time in their trailers or dressing rooms waiting to perform their scenes. Actors who perform in a television series often appear on camera with little preparation time, because scripts tend to be revised frequently or even written moments before taping. Those who appear live or before a studio audience must be able to handle impromptu situations and calmly ad-lib, or substitute, lines when necessary.

Evening and weekend work is a regular part of a stage actor's life. On weekends, more than one performance may be held per day. Actors and directors working on movies or television programs—especially those who shoot on location—may work in the early morning or late evening hours to film night scenes or tape scenes inside public facilities outside of normal business hours.

CASTING NOTICE: SHERRI'S STAGE

Sherri's Stage will hold eligible performer auditions for their 25th Anniversary Season, on Tuesday, Wednesday, and Thursday, September 3rd, 4th, and 5th at the Boone Audition Center. Productions will include *A Few Good Men*, *The Sunshine Boys*, *A Christmas Carol*, *Angels in America*, *Three Tall Women*, *Macbeth*, and *The Sisters Rosenzweig*. Please prepare a brief classical monologue.

The type of role being played often determines the amount of physical exertion required. For some roles, performers move about a great deal when walking or running, riding horses, dancing, or performing hazardous stunts (a professionally trained "stunt person" usually undertakes the more dangerous stunts).

Considerable traveling is often required of performers employed by theatrical road companies. These individuals perform the same play in a series of different locations. They frequently give an evening performance in one city and spend the following day traveling to the theater where their next performance is to be given. They must adjust to the varying facilities and equipment available in each theater. Movie personnel are also required to travel to sites that have been chosen as film "locations."

The physical surroundings of actors performing in stage productions can range from modern, air-conditioned, comfortable, and well-equipped theaters to those that are old and have inadequate facilities. Backstage areas of many theaters are crowded, dusty, drafty, and poorly ventilated. Actors may be provided private dressing rooms or apply their makeup and change costumes in areas shared by several other performers.

Training and Qualifications

Actors should possess a passion for performing and enjoy entertaining others. To gain experience, most aspiring actors participate in high school and college plays, work in college radio stations, or perform with local community theater groups. Local and regional theater experience and work in summer stock, on cruise lines, or in theme parks helps many young actors hone their skills and earn qualifying credits toward membership in one of the actors' unions. Union membership and work experience in smaller communities may lead to work in larger cities, notably New York or Los Angeles.

In television and film, actors typically start in smaller television markets or with independent movie production companies and then work their way up to larger media markets and major studio productions. Intense competition, however, ensures that only a few actors reach star billing.

Formal dramatic training, either through an acting conservatory or a university program, generally is necessary; however, some people successfully enter the field without it. Most people studying for a bachelor's degree take courses in radio and television broadcasting, communications, film, theater, drama, or dramatic literature. Many continue their academic training and receive a Master of Fine Arts (MFA) degree. Advanced curricula may include courses in stage speech and movement, directing, playwriting, and design, as well as intensive acting workshops. The National Association of Schools of Theatre accredits 128 programs in theater arts.

Actors, regardless of experience level, may pursue workshop training through acting conservatories or by being mentored by a drama coach. Actors also research roles so that they can grasp concepts quickly during rehearsals and understand the story's setting and background. Sometimes actors learn a foreign language or train with a dialect coach to develop an accent to make their characters more realistic.

The curriculum catalogue offered by the University of Illinois at Urbana-Champaign offers insights for prospective theater majors.

The curricular options in the Department of Theater provide intensive and extensive preparation for the rigorous demands of a professional career in the theater. A strong commitment to work in the theater and a realistic understanding of its intellectual, aesthetic, and physical demands are therefore necessary in students who enter the department.

Before acceptance in the undergraduate programs in theater, applicants must participate in auditions or interviews, which take place at the Krannert Center for the Performing Arts five or more weekends each year, and at selected regional locations (normally Chicago and New York). In these auditions, applicants who ultimately plan to pursue the curriculum in acting should present a three-minute audition, comprising two contrasting works from dramatic literature.

Applicants who wish to pursue a curriculum in design, technology, or management should present a portfolio of previous theater work. Applicants who intend to pursue the theater studies curriculum should also bring evidence of their previous theater work and a 500-word essay addressing the aspects of the theater studies program that interest them most and why they want to pursue those aspects. Information on these auditions and interviews will be sent to applicants once their admissibility to the University has been determined by the Office of Admissions and Records.

Three curricula are offered in theater: (1) the Professional Studio in Acting, (2) the Theater Studies Curriculum, and (3) the Division of Design, Technology and Management, which has specialized options in scene design, costume design and construction, stage management, theater technology, and lighting. Students are formally admitted to these curricula only after an evaluation by the faculty during the students' first or second year. The programs in acting and theater design, technology, and management are intended for students who, in the judgment of the faculty, are ready to concentrate in these specialties in an intensive undergraduate professional training curriculum. The theater studies curriculum is intended for students who plan to pursue advanced training and/or careers in directing, dramaturgy, playwriting, theater management, theater for social change, theater for youth, and theater history and criticism.

As one of the resident producing organizations of the Krannert Center for the Performing Arts, the Department of Theater produces six or seven fully mounted productions each academic year and three each summer. The theaters and workshops of the Krannert Center serve as laboratories for theater students, who have the opportunity to learn and to work alongside an outstanding staff of resident theater professionals and visiting artists, preparing performances in theater, opera, and dance. In addition, the department sponsors a small experimental theater space for student-directed productions.

All theater majors must successfully complete five production crew assignments at the Krannert Center under THEA 100-Practicum, I. Acting and theater studies students cast in Krannert Center productions or assigned to assist in Krannert Center productions must also take THEA 400-Practicum, II. Design, technology, and management students are required to work on Krannert Center productions as assigned for THEA 400-Practicum, II, credit. Students seeking credit for practical theater work outside the Krannert Center must secure the approval and supervision of theater faculty in the form of an Individual Project (THEA 391 or THEA 392) or as a Professional Internship (THEA 490).

Curricula in Theater

For the degree of Bachelor of Fine Arts in Theater, a minimum of 128 hours of credit is required.

First-Year Courses for All Theater Curricula

Hours	Required Courses
3	THEA 101—Introduction to Theater Arts
2	THEA 104—Introduction to Scenecraft
2	THEA 105—Introduction to Costume Technology
2	THEA 106—Introduction to Lighting Technology
2	THEA 107—Introduction to Stage Makeup
3	THEA 108—Dramatic Analysis
3	THEA 170—Fundamentals of Acting, I
3	THEA 175—Fundamentals of Acting, II, or THEA 125—Graphic Skills
20	Total

Professional Studio in Acting

The acting program provides intensive training in a wide variety of performing media. In the first and second years, students take introductory courses in movement, voice, and acting. In their second year of study in the department, students must audition for acceptance into the professional studio in acting. In addition to successful completion of all classes in their first and second years, acceptance will be based on an evaluation of each student's potential for professional-caliber performance, commitment to theater, and the necessary discipline for intensive study. Third- and fourth-year students meet in daily four-hour sessions, each of which includes sections in dynamics, voice and speech, movement, and acting. Semester-long acting sections include advanced scene study, musical theater, Shakespeare, and acting for the camera. Students in the professional studio in acting must audition for department productions and perform as cast.

Hours	General Requirements
4	Composition I
	Advanced Composition (fulfilled by THEA 261—Literature of Modern Theater)
6	Quantitative reasoning, I and II
0–12	Foreign language
18	General education
	Humanities and the arts (fulfilled by THEA 101 and 261)
6	Natural sciences and technology
6	Social and behavioral sciences
6	Cultural studies (Western and non-Western cultures)
12	General non-theater electives
8	General and/or professional electives
48	Total

Hours	Required Theater Courses
20	Required first-year theater courses
5	THEA 100—Practicum I
3	THEA 261—Literature of Modern Theater
3	THEA 270—Relationships in Acting, I
3	THEA 275—Relationships in Acting, II
2	THEA 276—Acting: Voice
2	THEA 271—Acting: Movement
8	THEA 371—Acting Studio I: Dynamics (2 hr.)
	THEA 372—Acting Studio I: Voice (2 hr.)
	THEA 373—Acting Studio I: Movement (2 hr.)
	THEA 374—Acting Studio I: Acting (2 hr.)
8	THEA 375—Acting Studio II: Dynamics (2 hr.)
	THEA 376—Acting Studio II: Voice (2 hr.)
	THEA 377—Acting Studio II: Movement (2 hr.)
	THEA 378—Acting Studio II: Acting (2 hr.)
8	THEA 471—Acting Studio III: Dynamics (2 hr.)
	THEA 472—Acting Studio III: Voice (2 hr.)
	THEA 473—Acting Studio III: Movement (2 hr.)
	THEA 474—Acting Studio III: Acting (2 hr.)
8	THEA 475—Acting Studio IV: Dynamics (2 hr.)
	THEA 476—Acting Studio IV: Voice (2 hr.)
	THEA 477—Acting Studio IV: Movement (2 hr.)
	THEA 478—Acting Studio IV: Acting (2 hr.)

Hours	Required Theater Courses
2	THEA 400—Practicum, II
4	THEA 461—History of Theater, I
4	THEA 462—History of Theater, II
80	Total

See Appendix A for additional information.

Once you have your degree and some basic experience, the best way to get started is to make use of opportunities close to you and to build upon them. For example, regional theater experience may help in obtaining work in New York or Los Angeles. Modeling experience may also be helpful.

Actors and actresses must have a sincere interest and affection for acting, as well as talent, training, poise, stage presence, the ability to move an audience, the ability to follow directions, an appealing physical appearance, and experience in order to succeed. Other important qualities include hard work, self-confidence, dedication, versatility, ambition, good health, poise, patience, commitment, stamina, the ability to memorize, the ability to withstand adverse conditions, perseverance, drive, determination, desire, discipline, and the ability to handle emotional tension and disappointment. Those who are self-conscious or withdrawn will not make it.

The length of a performer's working life depends largely on training, skills, versatility, and perseverance. Some actors continue working throughout their lives; however, many leave the occupation after a short time because they cannot find enough work to make a living.

Earnings

Minimum salaries, hours of work, and other conditions of employment are covered in collective bargaining agreements between the producers and the

---

CASTING NOTICE: SEEKING TALENTED ACTORS/VOICES

Deborah Casting Company wants you on file! E-mail abcdefgh@xxx.net for address to send headshots/résumé, and for information. We are located in Central Pennsylvania—a terrific location for production work in Harrisburg, Lancaster, Baltimore, Philadelphia, Allentown, and Reading. Great day work for professional actors who are experienced in teleprompter, commercials, and industrial scene work. We hope to hear from you soon.

CASTING NOTICE: *AN INSPECTOR CALLS*

The Rhinebeck Theater Society announces auditions for its production of J. B. Priestley's *An Inspector Calls*, to be held at the Rhinebeck Center for Performing Arts on Route 308 in Rhinebeck. Auditions will be held Saturday, August 28, from 1 to 5 P.M. and Sunday, August 29, from 10 A.M. to 1 P.M. Performances will be Thursday through Sunday, October 21, through November 7. The cast of seven requires one woman in her twenties, attractive and high-spirited; one man, approximately thirty, well-bred, privileged, but caring; two men in their fifties, both with imposing personalities; one woman in her fifties, strong-willed; one man in his mid-twenties, troubled and ill at ease; one woman in her twenties or thirties with few lines but an important physical presence throughout the play. Women may be considered for the inspector's role. English accents a plus but not mandatory.

unions representing workers. The Actors' Equity Association (Equity) represents stage actors; the Screen Actors Guild (SAG) covers actors in motion pictures, including television, commercials, and films; and the American Federation of Television and Radio Artists (AFTRA) represents television and radio studio performers. While these unions generally determine minimum salaries, any actor or director may negotiate for a salary higher than the minimum.

Under terms of a joint SAG and AFTRA contract covering all unionized workers, motion picture and television actors with speaking parts earned a minimum daily rate of $678 or $2,352 for a five-day week as of July 1, 2003. Actors also receive contributions to their health and pension plans and additional compensation for reruns and foreign telecasts of the productions in which they appear.

According to Equity, the minimum weekly salary for actors in Broadway productions as of June 30, 2003, was $1,354. Actors in off-Broadway theaters received minimums ranging from $479 to $557 a week as of October 27, 2003, depending on the seating capacity of the theater. Regional theaters that operate under an Equity agreement pay actors $531 to $800 per week. For touring productions, actors receive an additional $111 per day for living expenses ($117 per day in larger, higher cost cities).

Some well-known actors who achieve star status earn well above the minimum; their salaries are many times the figures cited, creating the false impression that all actors are highly paid. For example, of the nearly 100,000 SAG members, only about 50 might be considered stars. The average income that SAG members earn from acting—less than $5,000 a year—is low because employment is erratic. Therefore, most actors must supplement their incomes by holding jobs in other occupations.

Each motion picture is a separate entity and the terms may vary from one film to another. Some top stars receive a percentage of the box office sales along with their stated salary. Once agreed upon, contracts are drawn up that specify overtime and residual rights. (Residual rights are those payments made to actors or actresses for reruns of films, television shows, and commercials.) Sometimes performers may receive residuals for pay television, cable television, or videotape sales.

Many actors who work more than a set number of weeks per year are covered by a union health, welfare, and pension fund, which includes hospitalization insurance and to which employers contribute. Under some employment conditions, Equity and AFTRA members receive paid vacations and sick leave.

Career Outlook

Employment of actors is expected to grow about as fast as the average for all occupations through 2012. Although a growing number of people will aspire to enter the profession, many will leave the field early because the work—when it is available—is hard, the hours are long, and the pay is low. Competition for jobs will be stiff, in part because the large number of highly trained and talented actors auditioning for roles generally exceeds the number of parts that become available. Only performers with the most stamina and talent will find regular employment.

Expanding cable and satellite television operations, increasing production and distribution of major studio and independent films, and continued growth and development of interactive media, such as direct-for-Web movies and videos, should increase demand for actors. However, greater emphasis on national, rather than local, entertainment productions may restrict employment opportunities in the broadcasting industry.

Venues for live entertainment, such as Broadway and off-Broadway theaters, touring productions and repertory theaters in many major metropolitan areas, theme parks, and resorts, are expected to offer many job opportunities; however, prospects in these venues are more variable, because they fluctuate with economic conditions.

Strategy for Finding the Jobs

Armed with your college degree, basic knowledge of the acting business, and some experience, you'll need to prepare a portfolio that will highlight your qualifications, acting history, and special skills This will take the form of a résumé. You will also need to have photos taken by a professional photographer (one who shows you off to your best advantage). These are the essential tools of your trade. Attach your résumé to the back of your picture with one staple at both the upper left and right-hand corners. Once you have your portfolio ready, you can start "making the rounds" at casting offices, ad agencies, producers' offices, and agents. Several trade newspapers contain casting information, ads for part-time jobs, information about shows, and other pertinent data about what's going on in the industry. Among these are *Ross Reports* and *Back Stage* in New York and *Back Stage West* in Los Angeles. All three are available online at backstage.com. There is also the weekly *Variety*; in Los Angeles, there are *Daily Variety* and the *Hollywood Reporter*. These three publications are available at variety.com.

Once you drop off your résumé and head shots, you shouldn't just sit at home waiting for the phone to ring. It's wise to stay in contact—stop by and say hello. Check in by phone every week to see if any opportunities are available for you. If you are currently in a show, send prospective employers a flyer. It shows them that you are a working actor.

When you get past this initial stage and actually win an audition, here are some things you should remember:

Audition Tips
1. Be prepared.
2. Be familiar with the piece—read it beforehand and choose the parts you'd like to try out for.
3. Go for it—don't hold back.
4. Speak loudly and clearly—project to the back of the room.
5. Take chances.
6. Try not to be the one going first—if you can observe others you can see what they do, try to avoid their mistakes, and get a feel for the script.
7. Be enthusiastic and confident.
8. Keep auditioning—even if you don't get any parts, you are getting invaluable experience that is bound to pay off.

So when do you get an agent? Not right away, anyway.

First of all, you don't need an agent to audition for everything. There are many things you can audition for that do not require an agent—theater, nonunion films, union films. However, most commercials are cast through agencies, so you would most likely need an agent to land one of those.

While waiting to be chosen for a part, acting hopefuls often take jobs as waiters or waitresses, bartenders, taxi drivers, etc.—workers who are afforded a flexible schedule and money to live on.

Professional Associations

Actors' Equity Association
165 West 46th St., 15th Floor
New York, NY 10036
actorsequity.org

Alliance of Canadian Cinema, Television and
Radio Artists
2239 Yonge St.
Toronto, ON M5S 2B5
Canada
actra.ca

American Alliance for Theater and
Education
7475 Wisconsin Ave.
Suite 300A
Bethesda, MD 20814
aate.com

American Association of Community Theater
8402 BriarWood Crest
Lago Vista, TX 78645
aact.org

American Federation of Television and
Radio Artists (AFTRA)
260 Madison Ave.
New York, NY 10016
aftra.org

American Film Institute
2021 North Western Ave.
Los Angeles, CA 90027
afi.com

American Guild of Variety Artists (AVA)
4741 Laurel Canyon Blvd., Suite 208
North Hollywood, CA 91607

American Theatre Works, Inc.
P.O. Box 510
Dorset, VT 05251
dorsettheatrefestival.com

Canadian Actors Equity Association
44 Victoria St., 12th Floor
Toronto, ON M5C 3C4
Canada
caea.com

National Association of Schools of Theatre
11250 Roger Bacon Dr., Suite 21
Reston, VA 20190
nast.arts-accredit.org

Screen Actors Guild (SAG)
5757 Wilshire Blvd.
Los Angeles, CA 90036
sag.org

Theatre Communications Group (TCG)
520 Eighth Ave., 24th Floor
New York, NY 10018
tcg.org

A Close-Up Look at Actors

Acting provides career opportunities in so many different areas that it would be impossible to consider all of them in depth. Here are close-ups of three people who have selected various aspects of acting as their vocations.

Jennifer Aquino, Actor

Jennifer Aquino has appeared in television, movies, and stage productions. Her credits include the television shows "Weird Science," "Caroline in the City," "JAG," and "Twin Peaks." Jennifer's movie credits include *The Party Crashers*, *Prisoners of Love*, *Screenland Drive*, and *Ralph the Waiter*. She has performed on stage in *People Like Me* at the Playwrights' Arena; *Gila River* at Japan America Theater; and *Cabaret* and *Sophisticated Barflies* at East West Players. These are only a few of her accomplishments in all three media.

Jennifer is the lead voice of Catherine Stanfield in Microsoft and Genki's Xbox car chasing combat game Maximum Chase, and is the recurring voice of Chelsea in the new Rugrats animated series "All Grown Up." You can also see her in a national commercial for Home Depot.

Jennifer enjoyed performing for her family as a child and acted for the first time in elementary school. She received the Performing Arts Award in high school, and ultimately studied theater and dance at UCLA, graduating with a B.A. in economics. Her first break after graduation was playing Eolani in the television series "Twin Peaks," a job she won after her very first audition. Jennifer then got an agent and joined the Screen Actors Guild and continues performing in theatrical productions. She is a founding member of Theater West and the East West Players Network.

Like most actors starting their careers, Jennifer initially held a full-time job while pursuing her dream. She worked in the health-care industry for Kaiser Foundation Health Plan, and then as a health-care consultant for the accounting firm Deloitte & Touche. Jennifer was fortunate since, as she says, "I was such a good employee that my managers would be flexible and let me go out on auditions. After a few years, I realized that I was working too many hours (seventy to eighty per week), and I finally had to make a decision to quit my day job and focus 100 percent of my time toward acting. After booking a few jobs, including a national commercial, I was able to do so. It was a big risk, but one I felt necessary to take. I remember what my acting coach would say—'part-time work gets part-time results.' The more I put into acting, the more I got out of it."

As a full-time actor, Jennifer still maintains a very busy schedule. She works forty to sixty hours each week, either preparing for an upcoming job or audition, or interacting with agents and managers, and promoting herself to casting directors, producers, and writers. Jennifer is aware of the potential stress that can result from such a busy schedule, and also works hard at maintaining her health and having some time to relax.

Jennifer talks about the ups and downs of acting: "What I like most about my work is that I can say that I am making a living doing what I absolutely love to do, and that I am pursuing my passion in life. Not too many people in this world can say that. What I like least about my work is that there are a lot of politics in it. It's not always the best actor that gets the job. Some of the time, it's a certain look, what your credits are, who you know, etc., that determines who gets the job. There are a lot of things that are out of your control. That's just part of the business and you have to accept it."

Gonzo Schexnayder, Actor

Gonzo Schexnayder is an actor following a different path from Jennifer's. He has a B.A. in journalism and advertising from Louisiana State University in Baton Rouge, and has taken acting classes at LSU and Monterey Peninsula College in Monterey, California. In addition, he has attended Chicago's Second City Training Center and The Actors Center, and is a member of both SAG and AFTRA.

Gonzo's initial dream was to do stand-up comedy, but he did not pursue it until he graduated from college and began working with an improvisational comedy group. Within a few months he was on military assignment in Monterey, California, for language training. During this time Gonzo had his first show, and still recalls how happy the experience made him: "I'd never felt such elation as when I performed. Nothing in my life had given me the sheer thrill and rush that I experienced by creating a character and maintaining that throughout a given period of time. Nothing else mattered but that moment on stage, my other actors, and the scene we were performing."

Realizing how important it was for him to be happy with his work, Gonzo decided to pursue acting as his career. Although this meant working on his acting while also working at a more steady job, Gonzo was willing to make the commitment. As he says, "Sure I'd love to have an apartment with central air and a balcony. I'd love to have a car that is still under warranty. But I know that by putting my efforts and money into my acting career, those other things don't matter. . . . Cars and apartments don't give me the satisfaction that being an actor does."

Gonzo's schedule varies depending on the project he is involved in. He is a founding member of Broad Shoulders Theatre in Chicago, which takes a good deal of his time. He is also pursuing a voice-over/on-camera career, and attends classes and workshops toward that end.

Gonzo offers his views on the ups and downs of acting: "I love the process of acting and sometimes just the fast-paced, eclectic nature of the business. There is always something new to learn and something new to try. The sheer excitement of performing live is amazing, and the personal satisfaction of getting an audience to laugh or cry simply by your words and actions is very gratifying.

"I dislike pretentious actors and people who take advantage of an actor's desire to perform. As one of the only professions where there is an abundance of people willing to work for nothing, producers/casting directors/agents/managers who only care about the money will take advantage of and abuse actors for personal gain. Being an astute actor helps prevent much of this, but one must always be on the lookout."

Mike Matheson, Voice-Over Artist

Another career to consider is that of Mike Matheson, a full-time freelance voice-over artist. He has a B.S. in psychology from Lawrence University in Appleton, Wisconsin, and has been pursuing his career since 1985.

Music is a big part of Mike's background. He studied piano, drums, saxophone, and guitar, and performed in folk groups and rock bands during his high school years. Mike worked at a college radio station, where he learned about production, writing commercials, and voice-overs. After graduation, he worked as a professional musician, performing in clubs throughout the Midwest.

Mike's next job was at a small-market cable television station in Wisconsin, where he was talk show host, sports anchorman, advertising salesman, commercial writer and voice-over, cameraman, and telethon host. Mike describes this time as "the dues-paying years . . . a true learning experience. But it gave me a great deal of perspective regarding what was to come."

Mike eventually worked as a recording engineer in a studio that specialized in commercial production. Simultaneously, he pursued his freelance voice-over career. When he reached the point where he earned more money from the voice-over work, Mike decided to make it a full-time career.

The basis of Mike's work involves talking on radio and television commercials, and industrial films and tapes. His jobs are the result of auditions, previous employment, word-of-mouth recommendations, and submitting demo tapes.

Mike reads from a script, under the direction of a producer or copywriter. For television work, he reads to a video and his voice, music, and sound effects are then edited to the picture. Most of his work is done in Chicago recording studios, although his clients are located around the country. He occasionally travels if his client cannot go to Chicago or does not want the recording done by telephone.

Mike says that he does not have typical days, and so must provide his own structure and discipline to his schedule. As he says, "The need to 'keep an even keel' is, to me, the single most important aspect of my job. That is because of the unstable and volatile nature inherent in this field. There is very little predictability in the amount of work, income, time required, stress level, or in the personalities involved in my work. That can be both good and bad. The variety can be very stimulating as well as stressful."

On average, Mike spends about fifteen hours per week recording in the studio, and three or four hours auditioning. While this schedule might give him a good deal of free time, he must also be available on short notice when a new job opportunity occurs. For this reason, Mike says that "adaptability is an absolutely essential trait, and long-term planning is sometimes impossible. Making good use of free time is very important, because I never know when it might end."

Mike acknowledges that voice-over work can be extremely lucrative. While this is obviously a great benefit, it also increases the competition in the field, making marketing a very important part of the job. Mike estimates that he spends nearly 80 percent of his work week outside the studio, going to auditions or promoting himself.

Mike employs a three-step marketing strategy. He sends occasional mass mailings to 2,500 writers and producers at ad agencies in his market. He annually produces a voice demo tape that he sends to the same 2,500 people. The tape includes samples of his work edited into one tape. Finally, Mike employs a personal representative to make visits and calls on his behalf.

This busy and exciting job naturally includes some ups and downs.

Although Mike works steadily, he knows that his situation could change at any time. "It's hardly ever physically dangerous. The most dangerous thing is if something were to happen to prevent me from working. If I don't work I don't earn. If I became disabled, private disability insurance wouldn't begin to replace my earnings. There are no paid vacations. If I leave town, I might miss work that could potentially pay thousands of dollars. Learning to relax on vacations is a real art. I have to put lost income out of my mind so I can enjoy my time away.

"The other 'danger' is that my voice will somehow go out of style—that whatever people like about it will no longer be in demand. I've accepted that I really have no control over that. I've learned that all I can do is continue to remind people I'm available, give it my best when I'm called, and save my money when the big jobs come along; because, as one recording engineer said to me at the end of a recording session, 'You're fired again.' In some ways, that sums up my existence as freelance voice-over. Every time I finish a job, I'm unemployed again and in search of the next one."

Like many performers, Mike truly loves his work, and this benefit helps balance any negative concerns he might have. Mike says, "When I am hired for a job, I take great satisfaction knowing I've beaten the best in the business to get that job. The financial rewards pale in comparison to the joy I experience doing what I love. I feel blessed to have this job—one I am proud to say I do well. I love what I do. And, in spite of some of the pitfalls, I wouldn't trade it for any job in the world."

Advice from the Professionals

Jennifer Aquino's experience has led her to offer the following advice for aspiring actors: "I would advise anyone who is considering acting as a career to pursue your dreams and be persistent—but only if it's something you absolutely love to do, and there's nothing else in the world you would rather do. Pursue the creative as well as the business side of acting. Don't let anyone stop you from doing what you want to do. And always keep up your craft by continuing your training."

Gonzo Schexnayder offers his advice to anyone interested in his line of work: "I would advise others who are interested in this career to work where you are. Perfect your craft. Move when you 'have' to—you will know when it's time. And above all—trust your instincts."

To those considering a career in voice-over work, Mike Matheson has this to say: "I'd advise others to keep your seat belt fastened. Keep your shirt on. Keep your sense of humor. Keep your ego in check. Don't take anything personally—especially rejection. Keep your head. And when you make money, keep it. Remember when you're working, you're making more than anyone in the room. Make their job easy. Make them look good.

"Enjoy it. You're lucky."

Path 2: Behind the Scenes

When you were younger and taking part in performances, did you long to be the center of attention with all eyes focused on you, or did you prefer the idea of staying in the background helping with lighting, sound, and props? When you attend a performance, do you wonder about what's going on behind the scenes? Do you ever consider how many people it takes to ensure that everything on stage goes according to plan? Many people don't have any idea about what goes on behind the scenes and how many professionals perform a variety of tasks in order to make a performance as successful and entertaining as possible. In this chapter, you can explore what it would be like to become a part of the behind-the-scenes world of theater.

Definition of the Career Path

Team spirit is of the utmost importance for the professionals who work together behind the scenes to create performances everyone can be proud of. Those who work behind the scenes include stage directors, stage managers, technical directors, set designers, costume designers, hair stylists, makeup artists, lighting designers, sound designers, property designers, carpenters, scenic artists, wardrobe supervisors, special effects specialists, riggers, and broadcast technicians.

Stage Director
At the top of the stage hierarchy are stage directors, who are responsible for the creative decisions behind a production. Directors read each play to decide whether they are interested in directing it. If they decide to take on the pro-

CASTING NOTICE: SPECTACULAR PERFORMING ARTS

Spectacular Performing Arts is seeking professionals for part-time work: sound technicians capable of mixing live music, electricians familiar with boards, wardrobe and backstage personnel. Hourly rate is based upon experience. We are also seeking an assistant technical director, with sound, electrics, and rigging background.

This is a 20-hour workweek that pays $300. Medical benefits after 90 days. Please send your résumé to Spectacular Performing Arts Center, 2534 Tenth Street, New York, NY 10007, Attention: Ben Jones, technical director.

ject, they are in charge of coordinating the entire production of the play. The director meets with the playwright to decide about the best way to present the play. Additional conversations will take place with the producer about issues including casting, budgets, production schedules, designers, and other details.

Directors are the ones who interpret the plays or scripts as they see fit. They audition and select cast members, conduct rehearsals, and direct the work of the cast and crew. Directors use their knowledge of acting, voice, and movement to achieve the best possible performance and usually approve the scenery, costumes, choreography, and music.

Once directors have become familiar enough with the play to determine the approach and perspective they wish to take, they meet with designers to begin the process of creating costumes, scenery, sound effects, and lighting. With the aid of a stage manager, directors make hundreds of decisions in order to best represent the piece.

When rehearsals begin, directors are the ones who instruct the cast about where they are to be positioned on stage, how they are to move, and what feelings and actions they should display. In the process, they rehearse the performers as they practice their lines and make suggestions for changes whenever they see fit.

Upon presentation, directors often like to attend a dress rehearsal or preview and position themselves in different parts of the theater in order to observe the reactions of people in the audience. Even at that point, changes may be made—if the director feels they can improve the play.

Directors and producers often work under stress as they try to meet schedules, stay within budgets, and resolve personnel problems while putting together a production.

Stage Manager

Following the director, stage managers have the final say on most everything to do with the play and its production. Stage managers call the casts together to begin rehearsals. They see to it that everyone is present when required. They send an assistant to inform the stars when they will be needed and when to be ready to go onstage. If necessary, they make arrangements for stand-ins. They are the ones who give the signal for the house lights to dim, indicating that the production is about to begin.

Stage managers maintain a master script or a book containing all details of the play. The master script lists every actor's movements, entrance and exit cues, costume details, and lighting and sound cues. Any production changes are recorded in the master book.

Stage managers also maintain personnel records on all cast members and backstage workers including names, addresses, and contact information. They often have assistants who help with the backstage duties. If so, they are able to be out front to watch the play. In this way, they can stay attuned to changes or improvements that can be made.

Technical Director

Technical directors are assigned the task of coordinating all of the work of designers and their entire crews. They are responsible for making sure that all of the preliminary work moves forward on schedule and that everything fits together properly.

Technical directors meet with lighting, property, and sound designers to work out details. They also make sure that set changes and storage details work as planned. When on tour, technical directors aid other workers to make adjustments to fit the space and layouts of different theaters.

Set Designer

Set designers are entrusted with the responsibility of the physical environment of the play. To successfully accomplish this, they research the time and place of the play. Uncovering typical architecture for the play's time and place, they make sketches and models of possible sets and present them to the director for his or her approval. Then they make detailed drawings and models (exactly to scale) using cardboard, wood, plastic, clay, or other materials. The plans must show ways to prepare and move the pieces quickly and safely and how remaining sets may be stored offstage while one is being used onstage.

Set designers may meet with directors concerning details of construction costs and other relevant ideas. On the other hand, they may take their plans to two or three shops for bids. The designers then oversee the building and painting of the sets, whether this means creating stairs, mountains, balconies, or whatever is needed for the play.

Costume Designer

Costume designers must also conduct some research into the locale, period, and social background of the play, utilizing libraries and museums to study clothing styles and fabrication. Once this stage of designing is completed, they begin to draw sketches of costumes, which will eventually need the director's approval. Once approval is given, they bring the sketches to the theater costume shop to plan how to make them.

If the production is taking place in a large city such as New York, costume designers may secure bids from two or three costume shops. They select the fabric, approve the clothing patterns, and stay abreast of the progress of how the costumes are developing. For plays that will take place with a modern setting, costume designers might also shop for ready-made garments. If other pieces such as wigs or beards are needed, the costume designer will select them from a wig shop.

Once everything is secured, fittings are scheduled for cast members to make sure everything is right. And to ensure that everything looks the way it should overall, a dress parade is held under stage lights with scenery and props in place onstage.

Hairstylist and Makeup Artist

Hairstylists and makeup artists use cosmetics, pencils, greasepaints, brushes, and other materials to make the actors and actresses look like the characters they play. Makeup may also include hair, clay, or plastics to create wrinkles, warts, bald heads, tooth changes, burns, or scars. Even an actor's hands must be right for the character he or she is playing.

Lighting Designer

Lighting designers use lighting fixtures, patterns, color filters, and dimmers in order to create lighting effects. Referring to floor plans of the sets, they decide where to place each piece of equipment. The master electrician and lighting director plan the electric circuits for the equipment. The lighting board operator controls the lights in the theater throughout the play. Cue sheets will allow the operator to know exactly when to turn each unit on and off. In some cases, a computer in the light board handles these details, which expands the effects of lighting designs. In order to make sure that circuits and lights are in proper working order, lighting designers report for work one hour before the performance.

Sound Designer

Sound designers are the individuals who create and direct the making of sound effects: drumbeats, sirens, breaking glass, whirling tornadoes. The designers are faced with choosing and directing placement of amplifiers, speakers, synthesizers, microphones, and other equipment for maximum effect. Once satisfied with the results, cue sheets are made up for the sound-board operator to follow during all performances.

One or more sound technicians work during a show. One may work from a place in the audience mixing or blending the sounds the audience hears. Another, backstage, may control sounds the performers and musicians hear. A third worker may be in charge of handling prerecorded sounds or special sound effects. All wear intercom headsets to monitor the work going on at the time.

Property Designer

Property designers are involved in planning and, in some cases, directing the making of pieces needed for productions—anything from palm trees to antique sofas. Other items they may be asked to provide include books, violins, spears, shields, or a wide variety of other props. They may also be asked to construct masks or hands for characters appearing as dragons, monkeys, monsters, donkeys, or any number of other animals.

Carpenter and Scenic Artist

Working with materials such as wood, canvas, muslin, metal, clay, and other materials, carpenters and scenic artists are hired to build the sets and properties for a theatrical production.

Special Effects Specialist

Special effects specialists are the ones who create, plan, and install the devices needed to make smoke, rain, snow, fog, or other conditions that must be manufactured for a production.

Electrician

Electricians connect and mark the circuits for both sound and lighting effects.

Rigger

Riggers do their work considerably above ground level—hanging lighting, sound equipment, and scenery from wires and ropes. They are also involved in working with pulleys and counterbalances to control the movable parts of sets.

Broadcast Technician

Broadcast technicians operate and maintain the equipment used to record and transmit radio and television programs. They work with sound and video recorders, television cameras, transmitters, microphones, and equipment used for special effects.

Wardrobe Supervisor

Once the play opens, wardrobe supervisors are in charge of all of the costumes. Crews are hired to keep shoes polished, suits brushed, broken zippers replaced, hems stitched. Costumes may also need to be adjusted to fit stand-ins. When on tour, the wardrobe supervisors and their helpers are charged with packing and unpacking the costumes and putting them in the dressing rooms.

Possible Job Titles

Broadcast technician
Carpenter
Costume designer
Electrician
Hair stylist
Lighting designer
Makeup artist
Property designer
Rigger
Scenic artist
Set designer
Sound designer
Special effects technician
Stage director
Stage manager
Technical director
Wardrobe supervisor

Possible Employers

The same opportunities open to actors and actresses are generally available to those who work behind the scenes. This would include Broadway pro-

CASTING NOTICE: LYNNE COUNTY PLAYHOUSE

Lynne County Playhouse is seeking an experienced set designer to take charge of our production of *Romeo and Juliet* and direct several assistants. We also seek a carpenter for immediate hire, per show or full-season contract, and a sound designer/technician, beginning in August or September (possibly as a staff member). Competitive salary for all positions. Round trip and housing provided for set designer and carpenter positions. Please send letter and résumé.

ductions, regional plays, children's theater, summer stock, radio, television, and commercials.

Related Occupations

Related occupations include communications technicians, motion picture directors, script supervisors, program assistants (in radio and television), announcers, disc jockeys, and narrators. Others may be film editors, communications technicians, miniature set constructors, recordists, sound cutters, microphone boom operators, dubbing machine operators, or film loaders.

Other possible options include drama teachers, dramatic coaches, fashion designers, furniture designers, interior designers, artists' managers, booking managers, circus agents, and location managers.

Working Conditions

Working conditions for stage production workers will vary considerably, depending on the job. For instance, a musical on Broadway with a multi-million-dollar budget will differ greatly from a play with a cast of eight or ten in a small summer theater.

The physical aspects of the job may also vary greatly. Directors and designers generally spend a fair amount of time in an office or studio. A lot of time is also spent in empty theaters, which may be chilly, stuffy, drafty, or dark.

Most backstage workers are on their feet a lot. They move about both in the theater and out. They may be shopping around town for props, or visiting libraries or museums for research. Many hours are put in when a play is

CASTING NOTICE: *CABARET*

What good is sitting alone in your room? Come to the cabaret! The Ilene Theater in Madison, Wisconsin, is looking for a talented and enthusiastic Stage Manager for our fall production of *Cabaret*, with rehearsals starting immediately and performances scheduled for Friday and Saturday evenings and Sunday matinees for four consecutive weekends opening September 26. The Stage Manager will run all rehearsals and call all performances. This is a paid position. We already have a fabulous cast and crew. Please contact us.

in planning or rehearsal, with little thought given to schedules or working hours.

Costume and set designing crews often work in crowded areas constructing what is needed for the play. When the play is actually underway, many workers are in high-pressure situations, responsible for maintaining sets and costumes throughout every performance.

One issue of the utmost importance to all participants and the project at large is safety. There are a number of potentially dangerous situations—high-voltage equipment, hot lights, ladders with people climbing high or working on scaffolds. Safety laws are strictly enforced, however, and accidents are rare.

Training and Qualifications

Many schools have programs in fine arts, even at the middle school level and usually at the high school level. Students who plan to work in theater should take part in school plays and musical shows. High school students should take classes in history, literature, art, and English.

Hopefuls for careers behind the scenes should gain as much experience as possible working on productions in school, church, or local theater. Work done with a professional company is an added bonus. Working as a volunteer is also a good idea. Part-time possibilities include local theater, dinner theater, and special events like benefits or rock concerts.

Candidates for these careers should plan on earning at least a bachelor's degree in fine arts with a major in drama. Those who plan to focus on lighting and sound design may take courses in design, electricity, art, history, computers, electronics, mathematics, physics, and sound. Set designers may decide to major in architecture. They should take drawing, art and art history, drafting, and sculpture. Makeup artists must know something about anatomy. And they should also take sculpture, portrait painting, and other art topics. Most directors, stage managers, and designers earn a master of fine arts (M.F.A) degree in drama or another specialty, or a master of arts (M.A.) degree.

On a more personal level, it is important that directors and designers have a strong artistic sense along with the ability to make decisions and instill confidence in others. Managers who are organized, possess strong leadership skills, and can inspire teamwork are bound for success. Stage production workers need to be enthusiastic, energetic, confident, creative, and intelligent. They also need to have a good sense of humor and the ability to handle successes and failures.

Earnings

Earnings of stage directors vary greatly. According to the Society of Stage Directors and Choreographers, summer theaters offer compensation, including "royalties" (based on the number of performances), usually ranging from $2,500 to $8,000 for a three- to four-week run. Directing a production at a dinner theater generally will pay less than directing one at a summer theater, but has more potential for generating income from royalties. Regional theaters may hire directors for longer periods, increasing compensation accordingly.

The highest-paid directors work on Broadway and commonly earn $50,000 per show. However, they also receive payment in the form of royalties—a negotiated percentage of gross box office receipts—that can exceed their contract fee for long-running box office successes.

The following figures represent sample rates for summer theater jobs:

Stage directors—$500 to $2,500 a show
Stage managers—$150 to $350 per week
Costume designers—$500 to $1,500 a show
Set designers—$350 to $1,000 or more for each design

Lighting and sound designers—$110 to $330 or more per week
Property coordinators—$110 to $200 or more per week
Technical directors—$110 to $220 or more per week
Painters, carpenters, electricians—$110 to $330 or more per week
Wardrobe workers—$100 to $150 or more per week

Nearly all stage production workers belong to a union, maybe more than one. In New York City, Broadway and off-Broadway workers must belong to a union. In other locations, the requirements vary. Actors' Equity Association is a large, strong union to which actors and stage managers belong. Some theaters will only employ Equity actors or stage managers.

Behind-the-scenes workers may be paid by the week, month, or season. Those who are truly skilled at what they do, often get much more than a minimum amount. For example, though most riggers earn about $15 per hour, one who is experienced might get $3,000 for a single rock concert.

Sometimes summer theaters offer internships with a modest stipend. Some summer programs offer $500 to $900 for the season to assistant designers, stage managers, and technical directors. Technical production interns and shop assistants may be offered $75 per week.

Salaries for beginning, broadcast technicians in radio and television stations range from $190 to $330 per week. Experienced technicians earn $330 to $1,000 per week. Union technicians are entitled to union scale.

Career Outlook

Since the competition for jobs is so fierce, even seasoned workers have long periods between jobs. Although stage workers do have more steady employment than actors or dancers, many spend weeks and months at other jobs. It is an advantage if you can fill more than one slot—such as design both

---

CASTING NOTICE: TECHNICAL HELP

Seeking an experienced technician to build and rig scenery for the five remaining plays for this season with the Peter Power Repertory. Position requires budget management ability, strong carpentry, and stage rigging experience. Part-time, flexible hours. Pay $1,200–1,500 per production. Anticipated start, July 12. Please send your letter, résumé, and three references.

sets and props or make and remodel costumes as well as design them. This will increase your chances of finding work.

Strategy for Finding the Jobs

Although theater professionals aim to work on Broadway, there are many other excellent places to work as well. San Francisco, Los Angeles, Chicago, Boston, and many other cities have theater year-round. Regional and repertory theaters in all parts of the United States attract exceptional talent. Summer theater, dinner theater, and theme parks also offer opportunities.

Beginners often start as volunteers working as costume dressers, production assistants, and stagehands. Finding stage production work depends largely on individual effort and achievement. Being in the right place at the right time also helps.

Professional Associations

American Theater Works, Inc.
P.O. Box 510
Dorset, VT 05251
dorsettheaterfestival.com

**Association for Communication
Administration**
1765 N St. NW
Washington, DC 20036
aca.iupui.edu

Broadcast Education Association
National Association of Broadcasters
1771 N St. NW
Washington, DC 20036
beaweb.org

National Association of Broadcasters
1771 N St. NW
Washington, DC 20036
nab.org

National Association of Schools of Theater
11250 Roger Bacon Dr., Suite 21
Reston, VA 20190
nast.arts-accredit.org

National Cable Television Association
1724 Massachusetts Ave. NW
Washington, DC 20036
ncta.com

U.S. Institute for Theater Technology (USITT)
6443 Ridings Rd.
Syracuse, NY 13206
usitt.org

A Close-Up Look at Behind-the-Scenes Workers

As we have seen, many opportunities exist for those interested in working behind the scenes in theater. Here are accounts of some behind-the-scenes careers that might interest you.

Randall Presswood, Director of Performing Arts Facilities

Randall Presswood is Director of Performing Arts Facilities for Bloomsburg University in Bloomsburg, Pennsylvania. He earned a B.A. in technical theater from Coe College in Cedar Rapids, Iowa, and an M.F.A. in Theater Design/Lighting from Wayne State University. He served his internship as Assistant Technical Director at the Chelsea Theatre Center in New York City.

Randall became interested in theater while in high school, where he both performed and worked behind the scenes. As he says, "I enjoyed the challenge of solving technical problems for short-run productions that would enthrall, dazzle, or amaze the audiences. . . . It wasn't necessary for them to know that I had a part in this process—it was enough for me to know. Choosing theater as a career and lifestyle would allow me to experience this feeling day in and day out. For me, there was clearly no other choice."

In his current position, Randall has the opportunity to provide this same experience with his own productions, as well as offer a venue for other performers to present their work. Randall describes this as a "cycle of escape and entertainment: allowing others to fulfill their dream of providing joy for the theater-going public."

Lighting design interested Randall more than performing did, so he decided to study the field, and dreamed of one day accepting the Tony Award for outstanding lighting design (he admits that he still has his acceptance speech ready for that moment). Randall designed lighting for as many college productions as possible. During summers he worked as a theater technician, and every time insisted that he be allowed to design a production just to gain more experience.

Randall sought as much experience as possible, working in any available area of theater. He credits this with giving him a well-rounded education and valuable experience: "I learned what was needed as an actor to 'find the light,' what was needed to produce the light as a designer and electrician, and what was needed to make scenery safe, secure, pleasing, and exciting. I also learned what was needed to produce a costume on the stage and what was necessary to manage the stage during a production run. Everything I did added to a total education that has made it possible for me to conduct the business of directing a performing arts facility."

When he received his graduate degree, Randall accepted a position as a university technical director with lighting design responsibilities. He was asked to refurbish the university's production shop, which meant he had to research the replacement or purchase of all the shop's tools. He was later asked to design a student computer lab and refurbish the rigging, sound systems, lighting instrumentation, and lighting control. In addition, Randall had the opportunity to design a production space for a summer dinner theater.

Randall wanted to continue with facilities refurbishing, and looked for work in that area when he left the university. He ended up at a performing arts center still under construction in California. Randall was hired as Production Manager, responsible for all aspects of the production shop. He ordered every tool and cabinet, and worked in collaboration with theater and sound consultants in planning the new facility.

This new position added considerably to Randall's experience. He became familiar with lighting systems, stage carpentry, electrical systems, safety and fire codes, security issues, budgets, and personnel procedures. In addition, he freelanced as a lighting designer, scenic designer, and costumer, and joined Actors' Equity as a stage manager.

Randall had grown from a lighting designer to a theater designer, and wanted to pursue this career when he left California. He describes the shift in focus: "It's not that my career path had changed (after all, I was still a working theater professional), but it had evolved into what I had actually been trained for. All of my experiences contributed to one another, and my path as a theater designer (in hindsight) only seemed inevitable. It is these experiences, as much as my training, that landed me in my current position in central Pennsylvania as the Director of Performing Arts Facilities for Bloomsburg University."

Randall is responsible for two venues, a 600-seat hall and a 2,000-seat hall, and is expected to generate as much use of both as possible. On average, there are four classes and four performances or dress rehearsals each day in the two facilities. Events are scheduled a year in advance.

Much of Randall's time is spent on scheduling the many users who want to book productions in the two facilities. He carefully determines the needs of each user in an effort to help make the most of their use of the facilities. He reviews the technical rider for all outside groups who perform at the institution, and often contacts the groups to negotiate the technical aspects of a production.

The number of staff Randall employs depends on the performance season. The roster ranges from twelve to thirty assistants, who must be trained in the general practices of the facility, as well as the specifics of lighting and sound, and departmental and institutional policies and procedures. Often this training is done hands-on during performances, which requires a great deal of Randall's attention. He frequently works eighteen-hour days, and sometimes works for four to six weeks without a full day off. It is not unusual for him to be called to work during a weekend, although the usual schedule is eight to ten hours, Monday through Friday. Randall spends four to eight hours each week in meetings, and gives additional time to community involvement.

A good deal of Randall's time is spent planning for facility improvement, rehabilitation, equipment upgrades, and general maintenance. This aspect of the job requires a lot of advance planning and paperwork, and scheduling of professionals and union trades. Randall has to anticipate the needs of the facility and schedule work around the rentals and productions that generate income for the institution. To schedule effectively, he keeps abreast of current and proposed technology and theater trends, attending workshops, seminars, and conferences to gain this knowledge. Gaining the funding for these projects may require grant writing.

Managing a performance venue certainly has its ups and downs. As Randall says, "What I like most about my job is its constantly changing nature. Although I may do the same or similar work day after day, it is always for a new client with a new set of needs. The challenges are never ending, and the solutions to these challenges carry immediate and gratifying rewards. I am in a visible position. My success results in an increased demand on my time and talents. The more I am able to accomplish in my own venue, the more other venues come to me for advice or consultation. I accept this as a compliment and reward for my hard work. I am particularly pleased to be working for an institution that values my efforts, opinions, and proposals, and goes the extra step to secure the funding necessary for me to be successful. I have worked in places where this is not the case, so having that support and encouragement is a paramount reward.

"Of course the sometimes relentless hours and the need to occasionally function under 'crisis management' are among the dislikes of my job. As an administrator, I am sometimes viewed as the obstacle or enemy to those presenting in my venue. It is my job to provide a total experience for many users and patrons. However, each user is convinced that his or her four hours in my space is the most important thing I will do all year long. When I thoroughly research and propose a project and become convinced that it is an important step for the institution, it is indeed frustrating when I am unable to convince my superiors to accept that belief. The art of theater is a collaborative one, but the business of theater is often tooth and nail."

David Palmer, Theater Manager

David Palmer is Theater Manager of the Ruth B. Shannon Center for the Performing Arts at Whittier College in Whittier, California. He earned an A.A. in business at Delta College in Bay City, Michigan, a B.A. from California State University in Long Beach, and an M.A. and M.F.A. in stage lighting design, also from CalState. David also served two years at Michigan State University touring with the Ball of Yarns children's theater company and toured and taught in Lansing Public Schools with the Lansing Team of Four creative dramatics troupe. Other positions he has held include lighting designer, technical director, master electrician, instructor, and cofounder of a repertory theater.

David worked in the audiovisual department in high school, setting up lighting and sound for games and dances in the gym. Later a friend asked him to help on a summer production of a Gilbert and Sullivan operetta at a local community theater, and David worked on building sets for the show. He enjoyed the work and the sense of accomplishment it gave him. Once in college, David changed majors from business administration to theater, and since then has worked exclusively in theater.

David went to California to design the lighting for a touring opera, and found that a great deal of work was available there in theater. He transferred to California State University at Long Beach to complete his education, and credits the school's program with much of his success: "This program was simply outstanding, and provided significant professional training, contacts, and teaching experience. All of the jobs that I have gotten since coming out to California twenty years ago have been a direct result of the contacts that I began to establish when I transferred to CSULB."

David's job as theater manager is largely administrative. He spends a good deal of time on the telephone with artists, managers, printers, and potential donors. Most days he works on bookings and artist services, supervising the box office, marketing and public relations, technical preparations, and performances. Some days are busier than others, depending on the amount of time he must give to various tasks.

A typical day is from nine to twelve hours, six or seven days a week during the academic year. In the summer, the schedule reverts to a more typical nine-to-five, five days per week.

Since most of David's staff members are students at the college, he strives to maintain a work environment that is both professional and educational. "I find that I will spend ten or fifteen minutes explaining the 'why' of a question to a student, and helping the student reach a solution based on his or her own knowledge, rather than giving a definitive yes-or-no type of answer. The workplace is another classroom. As a result, the amount of work accomplished is often less than in a fully professional environment. But the students are gaining an understanding of a profession that is often perceived as being all play and no work. In the end, many of the artists and patrons that visit the Shannon Center are simply not aware that everyone on the crew is an undergraduate student."

David derives great satisfaction from his job. As he says, "First and foremost, I like watching the glow of an audience member's face as he or she exits the theater after a first-rate performance. I feel that I have helped accomplish something for each one of those individuals. Second (but not by much) is watching the expression of understanding light up a student's eyes as he or she suddenly discovers a new piece of information that has real-life application. After that, I enjoy meeting and working with all of the people—artists, patrons, students, staff. We are all in this together. This is a business of emotions, not just dollar signs. Everything has a human value associated with it."

Twyla Mitchell, Stage Manager and Teaching Assistant

Twyla Mitchell is a theater professional who can offer insight into two different careers. She worked as a costume shop teaching assistant as a method of paying for graduate school, and has also worked as a stage manager. Twyla studied in a combined M.A./Ph.D. program at the University of California at Santa Barbara, and earned her B.A. in drama from the University of California at Irvine. She also completed internships with the Pacific Conservatory of the Performing Arts in Santa Maria, California, and Western Stage in Salinas, California.

Twyla believes in the importance of educational theater. "First of all, it's one of the last remnants of truly experimental theater—while universities are concerned with making money, it isn't as all-consuming an issue as it is in the other forms of theater. Even students who do not go forth into the theater hopefully can come out with an appreciation for all it can mean—the importance of art in a culture that so often seems to have forgotten. On a more personal level, a professorship is likely to be a significantly more stable position than any other in theater."

The demands on a graduate student's time can be quite heavy. In Twyla's case, this included attending regular seminars, as well as doing additional reading on the week's topic. She was also expected to be involved in a side project, which involved from ten to thirty hours of work each week. A teaching assistantship took another twenty hours per week. Twyla says that a slow week involved forty hours spent on various projects. A typical week ranged from fifty to sixty hours. A hectic week, when papers are due or performances are pending, can involve eighty to a hundred hours of work.

Twyla truly enjoyed her work, despite the busy schedule. "I really love the classes I am teaching in the basic elements of costume-building. I never get tired of them. I also really love studying, researching, finding out things I never knew before and that maybe other people never knew before and trying to find clear, precise ways of explaining them.

"The downside is that there aren't enough hours in the week to do all that and spend time with my toddler, so I often find myself stretched terribly thin. I have tried to find shortcuts when I can—for example I do a great deal of research on the Internet, and often check out books in the one-hour blocks I get during the day to take home and look over after my child is in bed, but I still am forced to make many sacrifices in my attempt to reconcile all of these elements."

Twyla also enjoyed working as a stage manager, a position she describes as "professionals who know everything about what's going on and who get to call the shots. They seem to be the final authority on many issues."

A typical day for a stage manager generally involves attending meetings, whether small departmental meetings or large meetings with all of a show's designers. For a show in production, the stage manager has meetings with the actors and crew to check on their progress and to try to anticipate any potential problems. The stage manager writes up notes from the meetings and distributes them to others so that everyone is apprised of the status of the production.

Following meetings, a stage manager generally attends rehearsals, a performance, or perhaps both. In these settings, the stage manager might perform a number of duties, acting as stagehand or assistant when needed, depending on the size of the theater and the production.

The ups and downs of stage management, for Twyla, are the following: "The best part of being a stage manager is that you really have the opportunity to be in on all elements of the production, from concept meeting to post-show strike. You get to work with some truly amazing artists across the board and have a complete notion of the process.

"The downside is that with that comes the fact that the buck stops with you. As with all middle management, you are the one to whom the producers turn when a problem comes up, and you had better have a way of solving it. It can create a tremendous feeling of overload and pressure, which is why stage managers have a very high burnout rate. To paraphrase a cliché, when everything is going wrong, everyone blames you, and when everything is going well, nobody notices you."

Dennis Parichy, Lighting Designer

Another interesting career behind the scenes is that of lighting designer. Dennis Parichy earned a B.S. in theater from the School of Speech at Northwestern University in Evanston, Illinois. In addition, he completed course work in lighting design, drafting, drawing, and painting for the theater designer at Lester Polakov Studio and Forum of Stage Design. He works as a professional lighting designer.

Dennis became interested in lighting design while taking a college course in stage lighting. His teacher, Alvina Kraus, ran a summer theater program at Eagles Mere Playhouse in Eagles Mere, Pennsylvania, and agreed to bring Dennis there so that he could try his hand at lighting design.

Dennis worked on nine shows in ten weeks at Eagles Mere, serving as both electrician and designer. His only supervision or assistance came from the directors, an experience that let him use his knowledge from lighting class to light each show effectively and artistically. Dennis's only prior experience was working on the lighting crews of some university productions, so this challenge involved a good deal of trial and error.

Over the course of three summers, Dennis learned a great deal about transforming lighting ideas into effective designs. He learned to test each idea, and to figure out how to make it work with very limited resources. In the process, he also learned about his own lighting preferences.

This was a challenging process. According to Dennis, "It was, of course, a high-pressure situation guided only by my own insights and the needs of the moment. So compared to formal training, it was chaotic, but it gave me invaluable experience about the realities of achieving a lighting design. I was able to learn firsthand how you must light the actors and the space effectively in order to achieve the basic goal of making the theatrical performance visible to the audience in a way that helps them understand and relate to the onstage events."

Dennis describes lighting design as the ability to understand the nature of a script and find what emotions and images it evokes in you. Using the techniques of lighting design, these emotions and images are translated into ideas about color, direction, and intensity of light. Dennis breaks the job down into four major components:

1. **Experience the work.** This aspect includes reading a script, listening to a score, and/or watching a rehearsal in order to experience the work for yourself in some vivid and immediate way. This is when the lighting designer explores the ideas and emotions that the work arouses, and develops his or her own point of view about the work. Sometimes this process requires one reading, and sometimes many more are needed.

2. **Discuss the work.** The next stage focuses on discussions with the show's director and/or producer, the other designers, and anyone else involved in creating the overall production. This usually requires several meetings or phone conversations to determine the lighting, scenic, costume, and directorial needs of the show. The goal is to produce a unified approach to the play in which the lighting design will blend with and support the work of everyone else. This process takes place over the course of several weeks.

3. **Arrange the lighting instruments.** The third stage of the design process involves creating the actual plan for the lighting that will create the agreed upon effect. At this point, the lighting designer works at the drafting table and computer to analyze scenic elements of the production. The designer decides what kinds of lights are needed (or how to use those available), where to put them, where they will be focused, how to control them, and what color and intensity they must have in order to achieve the desired goals. The designer then has to produce a light plot, hookup, shop order, and other lists and specifications that will communicate to the crew what he or she needs, where it should be located in the theater, and how it will be wired and

equipped. This part of the job may be done by the designer himself or herself in the studio (or with assistants), and can last anywhere from a day or two to three weeks (for a large and complex show) and may require constant consultation with the producers, managers, and the shops that supply the equipment, and the men and women who do the installation.

4. **Create the lighting.** The last phase of lighting design is the actual week to several weeks spent in the theater creating the specific lighting and executing the design in order to give the show the desired look. This begins when the lights are hung and includes focusing the lights, creating the cues, rehearsing the show, and modifying and refining the looks so that they all help the audience experience the show. This phase usually takes two or three days for summer stock to about ten days for most regional theater shows and most plays. However, in the case of new and complex musicals, several weeks of twelve-hour days might be required.

Dennis finds it difficult to describe a typical day in his job, because every production has its own schedule and it is not uncommon for a professional lighting designer to design several shows at once. As he describes it, "A typical day might easily involve working in the studio in the morning on the light plot or hookup of a show you are going to do in two or three weeks. Then in the afternoon, you might go to a run-through of the show that you will light next week. During the rehearsal, you note important things about cueing and staging that must be taken into account. You may discuss specific cues, problems, or needs with the stage manager and director. At the end of rehearsal, you might be required to attend a production meeting about a show that you will do two months from now and discuss with the director and perhaps other designers various ideas about that show, what its 'story' is, and what it should look like. And then in the evening—if you're very busy and the schedule is tight (as it often is)—you either go home and read the script for another show or think about the show just discussed or go to the theater and begin focusing next week's show (until midnight, typically).

"There are of course an infinite number of variations on this schedule. The designer is required to take control of his or her work, to be independent, self-motivated, dedicated, and ambitious. You have to get the job done and no one is supervising you."

As in many aspects of theater, deadlines and schedules are an unavoidable part of the job. The show must go on, regardless of the designer's schedule or any other commitments. Postponements are not a possibility, and the lighting designer must be willing and able to work under as much pressure as occurs. In order to maximize their earnings, many lighting designers take on as many shows as they can fit into their schedules, adding to the high pressure of the job.

Dennis talks about the ups and downs of his career: "What I like most about my work is the chance to help create an effective theatrical event in collaboration with other eager, exciting, and stimulating theater artists. The process of creating the design—especially the days in the theater—is almost always an exciting and satisfying time, because it gives me a chance to exercise my skills and visual talents, which is immensely satisfying. The process— from show to show—may be bumpy or difficult or fraught with occasional conflict, but is almost always in the end such a source of fulfillment that this makes the difficulties acceptable.

"The downside of lighting design (applicable I believe to almost all theatrical careers) is that there is often a lack of continuity, security, and stability in theatrical work. No matter how advanced your career, there is always the possibility that you may have to struggle for sufficient work to support yourself and a family; as associates and colleagues move on in their careers you may have to unexpectedly develop new relationships and find new sources of work. Since the network of friends and professional colleagues— especially directors—is extremely important to one's success, you are often vulnerable to significant changes in your relationships with theaters and other theater artists. At some point, finding work that will stimulate and stretch your artistic muscles may be difficult, and you have to be continually aware of the need to escape from the typecasting that inevitably happens and to find ways to expand your horizons."

Mark T. Simpson, Lighting Designer

Mark T. Simpson is an up-and-coming lighting designer. He earned his B.A. from Case Western Reserve University in Cleveland, Ohio, and an M.A. from the American University at Washington, D.C., in interdisciplinary studies (lighting and set design for the theater). He is completing his M.F.A. in lighting design from New York University, Tisch School of the Arts. Mark also served an internship as stage manager at the Cleveland Play House in Cleveland, Ohio, and is now employed as a lighting designer.

Mark's interest in theater began in college, when he took an acting class as an elective and signed up for running the crew for extra credit. He became hooked on theater, and although he wasn't sure what job he might do, he knew he would work in theater in some capacity. As Mark describes theater, "It was the only place I'd ever been that the prospect of spending my time and exerting my energies didn't seem like intolerable drudgery. The theater was also filled with the nicest, most selfless people I had ever met."

Lighting design enables Mark to use all of his talents and interests, such as technology, art, mathematics and physics, and computers and robotics. In addition, Mark felt a personal attachment to theater. As he says, "theater as an art appealed to me politically and socially. It is an optimist's art form—that people can be changed and educated by peaceful demonstrations of opinions and alternatives. It is a pacifist's art form—it provides a socially acceptable outlet to explore and cathartically deal with violence and negativity—it never has the intention to harm the participants or the audience. It is an art form for people seeking to live healthy, whole, productive, creative lives."

Mark describes his typical day as involving "at least eight hours of doing something else that's not my career." In New York, Mark works a full day as a temp, doing clerical or computer work. As the resident designer for an equity summer theater, he also works as a carpenter. When he is working on lighting design, he also works as an electrician.

During the summer, Mark works three 40-hour weeks and one 100-hour week. Approximately eighteen hours of that time is spent as a lighting designer. "So, on the average," Mark says, "I have to work about ten hours for the privilege of working one hour on my career."

When he is working as a lighting designer, Mark spends about eight hours on drafting designs and doing paperwork, three hours in meetings, and eight to fifteen hours in rehearsals setting up the lighting design. It is the actual work in the theater that he likes best. As Mark describes it, "It is very busy, very tense, but not negative. I often am convinced that it's impossible to finish in time for opening, but I always do. I sometimes find myself crawling along ductwork twenty feet off the floor, or balancing a 200-pound pipe on a hydraulic lift twenty feet off the floor, but that is work that will go away once I reach the top of my profession. Being a lighting designer isn't dangerous, but getting there is.

"The work atmosphere is very positive. When you get in the theater and see a moment of magic on the stage that is a direct result of your effort and imagination, you hear immediate approval from your peers, and your spine tingles with the realization that this personal success of yours adds to the value of everyone else's work. And when an audience responds to it, your spine tingles again."

Mark describes his likes and dislikes about his work: "What I like most are the people, the creativity, ingenuity, problem solving, and short-term nature of projects. What I like least is the low pay, understaffing, under-budgeting, lack of time allotted for first-class work, and the poor public understanding of what constitutes high-quality work."

Sheila Quinn, Operations Manager

In addition to those who manage theaters and design shows, some professionals work in the supply side of theater. Sheila Quinn is Operations Manager at Syracuse Scenery and Stage Lighting Company, Inc., in Liverpool, New York. She earned a B.A. in technical theater from SUNY at Oswego, New York. She also served in summer stock with the Cortland Repertory Theatre in Cortland, New York; regional theater with the Alliance Theatre in Atlanta, Georgia; and with C. Henning Studios in Atlanta.

Although she began as a performer, Sheila's interest later changed to working behind the scenes. Her fascination with how things worked backstage combined with good mechanical skills made the transition seem natural to her.

Coming from a small town, Sheila didn't expect that she would find a career working in theater. She attended a community college, earning an associate's degree in criminal justice. Soon after, the Summer Cortland Repertory Theater opened, and Sheila discovered that most of the technical staff there either taught in the Theater Department or were technical theater majors at SUNY Oswego. She applied to the program at once. After graduation, Sheila moved to Atlanta to work as a stage carpenter at the Alliance Theater. She worked long hours and on weekends, but enjoyed the work nonetheless. While with Alliance Theater, she also worked part-time with a production company that handled corporate meetings and trade shows, and found that she enjoyed working in the corporate end of theater.

Sheila was hired by C. Henning Studios, a company that built large convention displays, provided lighting for corporate meetings and shows, and produced theme parties throughout the country. She had not taken any business courses, so most of her business training and experience was acquired on the job. Sheila credits her boss with teaching her enough to give her a solid business education. After six years, she decided that the eighty-hour workweek was no longer possible for her to maintain, so she returned to upstate New York and began working for Syracuse Scenery and Stage Lighting.

Sheila now works forty to forty-five hours each week, and spends much of her time in curtain sales. She sells by telephone or on-site visits, often visiting a facility to measure the stage and consult about the available options. She spends the majority of her time in the office, quoting prices for stage curtain projects.

Sheila also coordinates the manufacture of the stage curtains and installation of the stage rigging and lighting. The company generally has between fifty and sixty large jobs in progress simultaneously. These projects may take from six weeks to two years, from order to completion. In addition, there are usually several smaller jobs in production each week.

Overall, Sheila finds more positive aspects than negative in her job: "For the most part, the atmosphere is very relaxed. Our schedule gets very hectic from May to December, and summers can get particularly crazy. I enjoy working with some interesting individuals, and, like most companies, it's a very diverse group. Because we are manufacturers and installers, not everyone's background is in theater. Our sewing room is filled with skilled sewers and cutters with backgrounds in the garment and fur business. A lot of our production installation staff includes ex-roadies from the world of rock and roll, and the office staff has backgrounds in either theater or business. It makes for a very interesting mix.

"I love to travel, so when I am on the road making sales calls I am happiest. We also have begun to do some interesting projects for cruise ships, theme parks, and large performing centers, etc. I like these because they offer a challenge to our creativity. They usually require entirely different types of curtains and glitzier fabrics—not just your basic black curtain masking.

"I also enjoy the daily interaction with the variety of customers that call. However, sometimes quoting prices for stage curtains can become very mundane. The majority of stage curtains are the same, with only the sizes or the fabrics changing, so there is very little creativity to that part of my job. However, one of the things that makes my job interesting is that I have to wear a lot of different hats."

Advice from the Professionals

Randall Presswood offers some advice for anyone interested in a theatrical career: "If you want to make a living in theater, be prepared to go where the path leads you. Don't force yourself down the straight path when the winding one is tugging at your bootstraps. If it is important to you to be a theater professional, then just be in the theater. Don't insist that you become an actor or designer. Be willing (and prepared) to become a box office manager, stage carpenter, or a director of performing arts facilities."

David Palmer's advice to aspiring theater professionals is to love your work: "In order to be successful in this (or any) business, you must have a passion for what you do. That passion will help you strive for the best 100 percent of the time. An attitude of 'that's good enough' just isn't acceptable. Being an idealist who is capable of thinking in a geometric or nonlinear fashion is a big plus. Taking an idea, rolling it around and coming up with four more ideas that then spark four more ideas is how you come up with fresh and exciting events. Never say no until you have exhausted all of the possibilities, because if you really want something you will find a way of doing it.

Finally, always remember 'what goes around, comes around.' That favor that you do for someone else will come back to you just when you need it most. I have found that it has worked for me since the early 1970s, when I did that favor for my friend and helped him out with the Gilbert and Sullivan operetta."

Twyla Mitchell can offer advice on two fronts. To those interested in teaching, she says, "I would advise others to read as much as you can—not just plays but criticism and theory. Absorb all you can, whenever you can. Talk to 'people in the know' and glean as much knowledge as you can from them."

Twyla's advice for anyone interested in working as a stage manager is to be well-rounded: "I would advise others to learn all you can about the different aspects in theater—costumes, props, light, sound, acting, directing, etc. The more you know, the more effectively you can communicate with the artists you will be working with. It's also a good idea to brush up your self-confidence and self-esteem, because sometimes both can take a beating out there."

Dennis Parichy has some advice for anyone considering a career in lighting design: "I think the most important advice I could give someone interested in lighting design as a career is to be realistic about the likely monetary and artistic rewards of lighting design in the theater. If you have the dedication, drive, and ambition to tackle the professional world, to put in the inevitable apprenticeship of learning the ropes and living hand-to-mouth for a while, you have a chance. If you are determined to do it, and are willing to brave the rigors of finding your niche, you have a good chance of succeeding. Training is important, but dedication and enthusiasm, a willingness to learn and expand, a genuine enjoyment of and eagerness to work with and for others, and an effort to submit your artistic impulses to the needs and demands of the production are what will make you a success."

Mark Simpson has some honest advice for future lighting designers: "If you have to do this—you'll know it. Just show up and work hard. If you can, go to Yale or New York University—if you can't, don't give up. Visit with a number of other designers, decide what you like, and imitate it until you understand it. Take chances with your work. Make big statements as often as you can. Pay attention to the whole first, the details second. Leave yourself time to finish your designs, finished and modest is better than unfinished and grandiose. Draw every day. Paint every day. Draft every day. Have fun—why else would you be in this business?"

Sheila Quinn has some good advice for others interested in the business end of theater: "Even though I spend most of my day quoting and discussing curtains, I still have to be able to answer other questions about makeup, paint, color media, hardware, etc. So my first advice to anyone wanting to get into the business side of the theatrical industry is to make sure your educational background is well rounded in all phases of technical theater.

"The best advice I could give anyone would be to find an interesting production job, like a cruise line, theme park, or production company. There are so many more opportunities out there today. I would have loved to have traveled more before settling into a nine-to-five job. While you're still young and not tied down to family or other responsibilities, have some fun with your career."

8

Path 3:
The Business of Theater

"If you want something from an audience, you give blood to their fantasies. It's the ultimate hustle."
—MARLON BRANDO

Perhaps the world of theater is attractive to you, but not as a performer. Do you have a flair for business and enjoy management? Can you speak persuasively? Do you like to solicit money for worthwhile projects? Are you good with figures? Do you like to represent others? Do you enjoy working with people? Then the business of theater, with its wide array of career opportunities, might offer the perfect career path for you!

Definition of the Career Path

Those who are involved in the business of theater include producers, casting directors, theatrical agents, general managers, company managers, box office managers, house managers, touring production managers, and theatrical press agents (among others). All of them remain behind the scenes (as do the professionals in Chapter 7), but instead of attending to things backstage, they focus on theater as a business.

Producers
Producers are entrepreneurs who oversee the business and financial decisions of a motion picture, made-for-television feature, or stage production. They select scripts, approve the development of ideas for the production, arrange financing, and determine the size and cost of the endeavor.

Producers must find investors who are willing to put up money to finance the project. It is the producers who are ultimately responsible for turning a profit for the investors, so a great deal of responsibility comes with this position.

There are a number of ways for a producer to find a script. Playwrights may send them to producers; sometimes producers might also put on new versions of previous productions; and often the producer may commission a playwright to write a script. Once a script is located or written, the producer will pay the playwright for an option to use the script for a specified time period.

Producers hire or approve the selection of directors, principal cast members, and key production staff members. They also negotiate contracts with artistic and design personnel in accordance with collective bargaining agreements and guarantee payment of salaries, rent, and other expenses. Producers have many responsibilities—ultimately they are the ones who make the decisions that determine the success of the project.

Television and radio producers determine which programs, episodes, or news segments reach the air. They may research material, write scripts, and oversee the production of individual pieces. Television producers are employed by television stations or networks. Network television series usually have an executive producer who does the long-term planning for the show. Movie producers are employed by a film studio or may work independently. Theatrical producers work independently.

Producers in any medium coordinate the activities of writers, directors, managers, and agents to ensure that each project stays on schedule and within budget.

Casting Directors

Casting directors are influential theater professionals who audition and interview performers for specific parts in a play or movie. To correctly match people with parts, casting directors read scripts and then work with others in the production staff to determine their thoughts, ideas, and desires regarding the character's personality, voice quality, and physical appearance.

Casting directors may find the right performer in a number of ways. They develop advertisements and place them in the trades, newspapers, or other publications. These ads announce the casting requirements of the production. They may also hold open auditions where hundreds or even thousands of hopeful actors and actresses come to audition for parts. Most casting directors also have a file of information on all the performers who ever auditioned for them, as well as a file on those who have sent résumés and photos but have never formally auditioned.

In some cases, established actors or actresses hear about a production, are interested in a specific role, and instruct their agents to call the casting director. If these well-known actors and actresses are very successful in the industry and are right for the part, they will often get a role without auditioning. Similarly, casting directors might have a specific actor or actress in mind for a part. In these instances, they contact the performer's agent to check out the interest and availability.

Often casting directors and actors meet in a "pre-read session." Usually, this includes about twenty people who are in contention for the part. The purpose of the meeting is to screen out people so that the producer's time is not wasted unnecessarily. Usually, five or six candidates are chosen from the twenty to attend a "producer's session," which also includes the casting director.

Internships always provide invaluable education and experience. If you can secure a position as a casting director's intern, one of your important responsibilities might be to handle calls from producers and directors. You might also be involved in casting a TV show, which would require that you spend your days reading a script in order to determine the list of characters needed to fill these parts. Then you might send the list to agents (possibly also to Breakdown Services, who forwards them to agents and managers) who will subsequently send you submissions (envelopes with pictures and résumés of candidates) to fill these roles. Then you'd pick out the people to audition.

Agents

Agents are representatives who advise their clients in a certain area of expertise. They may represent athletes, writers, models, actors, producers, performers, and other types of celebrities. There are three types of agents who represent performers—commercial agents, theatrical agents, or full-service agents. Theatrical agents handle movies, television, and stage roles. Commercial agents handle only commercials. Full-service agents handle both. Also, agents may or may not be franchised. A franchised agent is one who is licensed to represent union performers.

Most theatrical agents work for large agencies that service many clients. They always use their contacts and are on the lookout for news about new plays or other projects so they know where and when actors will be needed.

Since it is true that an agent won't survive if his or her clients are not successful, they may also see to it that the actors they represent study acting, speech, voice, and dance—anything that will enhance their ability to get successful roles. It is in an agent's best interest to help make clients successful because substantial income is available for any agent whose clients strike it rich.

An agent spends most of the day on the telephone: negotiating, networking, arranging meetings, discussing prospects, maintaining connections, and keeping in touch with the industry trends and deals. Nearly one-third of all phone time is spent with clients, explaining what the agent is doing on their behalf and strategizing. Face-to-face meetings are also important. An agent has to be willing to find creative compromises and live with them. Those who are successful must have tenacity, the willingness to fight for their clients, and the ability to sell ideas effectively and communicate clearly.

General Managers

General managers are the professionals in charge of legal details. They may set up the play company as a corporation and also negotiate contracts with those who have been hired to be part of the production. They may aid in preparing budgets and make sure that costs stay within them. It is their job to set ticket prices, hire a company manager, and order the printed tickets.

Company Managers

Company managers are in charge of making out the payroll and seeing to it that appropriate taxes are paid. They also work with box office managers on receipts and ticket sales. Once the show is closed, they make sure that nothing remains in the theater.

Box Office Managers

Box office managers are strictly in charge of tickets. It is their job to arrange the sale of tickets through mail order, advance ticket sales at the theater, and any other available outlets. They are held accountable for all ticket sales and money derived from them.

House Managers

House managers are responsible for the upkeep of the theater. As a result, they must be present whenever anyone else is there. They are also in charge of ushers, fire and safety laws, and extra stagehands who are hired to move the sets into and out of the theater.

Touring Production Managers

When the show is on the road, touring production managers are in charge of all business affairs of the company. Their duties usually include obtaining local permits, hiring local stagehands, arranging for housing for the cast and other members of the staff, and working with local unions. They also audit box office accounts and write out and disburse paychecks.

Theatrical Press Agents

Theatrical press agents are the professionals in charge of handling all of the publicity for regional theater group productions, off-Broadway shows, and Broadway shows. For a show to be successful, it is imperative that enough publicity is organized so that sufficient ticket sales will be generated. To accomplish this, theatrical press agents must create press kits, prepare biographies, write press releases, arrange interviews, and deal with all media sources.

For this job, it is critical to make the right media contacts, which entails compiling lists that will be used to send press releases, press passes, and perhaps invitations for opening night. Additionally, the theatrical press agent must plan as many events and press conferences as possible to generate as much publicity as possible. It is important that these professionals are creative in developing new ideas and new angles for exposure through reporters, entertainment and feature writers, and other newspaper and magazine writers.

Opening night is a gala event run by the theatrical press agents. It is their responsibility to call all reviewers and critics on the day of the show to make sure they will be present in the audience. The agents will be on hand on the day of the opening to be the liaison to the media, to pass out press kits, or provide any information that is required.

Some theatrical press agents work alone; others have apprentices who work with them, helping them with their various projects.

Possible Job Titles

Advertising manager
Agent
Business manager
Casting director
Executive director
Fine arts manager
Managing director
Marketing director
Personal manager
Press director
Producer
Producing director

Production assistant
Publicist
Public relations director
Talent manager
Theatrical agent
Theatrical press agent

Possible Employers

The majority of employment opportunities exist in large, culturally active cities such as Los Angeles; Hollywood; New York; Chicago; Washington, D.C.; Philadelphia; Atlanta; San Francisco; and Toronto.

Producers may work in a number of settings. Those working in legitimate theater are self-employed. Some may be on the staff of not-for-profit theatrical companies, regional theaters, etc. Since they may produce any of the following—Broadway plays, off-Broadway plays, off-off-Broadway plays, road company productions, dinner theater productions, cabaret theater productions, regional theater productions, stock productions—they may find work in any of these situations.

Not all productions employ casting directors. Some utilize the services of the director or producer to handle casting responsibilities. Casting directors may work on a consulting basis, for a production company, or be on staff at a theater.

Related Occupations

The connections agents make in their careers come in handy if they decide to leave this line of work. Many enter the field their clients are in, such as producing, editing, publishing, and in rare cases, writing and directing. Other related professions include public relations, sales, labor relations, advertising, management, communications, and media relations.

Working Conditions

Professionals involved in the business of theater usually work in an office environment, but may spend little time there. They often work long hours, traveling extensively to conduct meetings with interested parties and attend plays and other productions. The pace is usually very hectic. A good deal of time is spent meeting people at parties and receptions, often on evenings and weekends.

Training and Qualifications

No standard educational or training requirements exist for most business theater professionals. However, a thorough knowledge and understanding of theater is absolutely necessary, and a college degree gives individuals a certain measure of credibility and increased opportunities for hands-on training. Course work should focus on theater, film, business, English, fine arts, law, fiscal management, and personnel management. Advanced degrees are generally not necessary and, as a rule, do not affect earnings. Seminars and workshops in theater and producing are important.

Professionals in this area of theater need good business sense, financial management skills, organizational skills, effective communication skills, strong interpersonal skills, and negotiation skills. They must also have the ability to listen, to match people with roles, to work under pressure, to relate to clients, to handle stress, and to attend to details.

There are no specific training requirements for producers. They come from many different backgrounds. Talent, experience, and business acumen are important determinants of success for producers. Actors, writers, film editors, and business managers commonly enter the field. Producers often start in a theatrical management office, working for a press agent, managing director, or business manager. Some start in a performing arts union or service organization. Others work behind the scenes with successful directors, serve on boards of directors, or promote their own projects. No formal training exists for producers; however, a growing number of colleges and universities now offer degree programs in arts management and in managing nonprofits.

A three-year apprenticeship with a member of the Association of Theatrical Press Agents and Managers (ATPAM) is required for theatrical press agents. While a college degree is not a requirement, many in the business feel that it is the best approach. Good course choices include public relations, communications, writing, advertising, marketing, business, English, and theater arts. Theatrical press agents must be creative, detail oriented, and aggressive and must have excellent verbal and written communication skills. They need experience in publicity, public relations, or promotion.

Earnings

In general, the pay for producers is good but varies based on experience, company, and production budget. Though producers on staff usually receive a specific salary, others do not. Instead, they might receive a finder's fee for putting together a group of investors. Others are compensated with a percentage of the profits earned from the show. Figures for producers can vary from a few thousand to hundreds of thousands of dollars.

Median annual earnings of salaried producers were $46,240 in 2002. The middle 50 percent earned between $31,990 and $70,910. The lowest 10 percent earned less than $23,300, and the highest 10 percent earned more than $119,760. Median annual earnings were $56,090 in motion picture and video industries and $38,480 in radio and television broadcasting. Those who belong to trade unions generally receive paid vacation and health insurance.

Because of the nature of the job, it is difficult to determine annual earnings of casting directors. A lot depends on whether professionals are consultants or on staff, the nature of the production, and how many productions they cast each year. For individuals who are on staff, salaries may range from $10,000 to $75,000 and up. Consultants may charge $2,000 to $40,000 or more per production.

Agents usually make a standard 10 or 15 percent commission of all of the client's earnings, but actual salaries vary greatly depending on the experience and talent of the individual. Agents working on a part-time basis can earn anywhere from $15,000 to $50,000 a year. Benefits vary. Agents working for large agencies generally are offered health insurance and paid vacations.

Because individuals are usually hired for specific productions, it's difficult to determine annual earnings for theatrical press agents. Factors affecting this include the number of projects that year, how long the production lasts, and the size and type of theater. Minimum earnings are negotiated by the ATPAM, an AFL-CIO union. Earnings include a minimum weekly salary plus a percentage for pensions, "vacation pay," and a set figure for a welfare fund. Theatrical press agents usually earn about $600 to $1,600 per week and up.

Career Outlook

The number of producers is small, and few new ones are hired each year. Theatrical producers work from show to show. For agents, success lies in finding new talent and promoting it in order to earn a reputation and a bigger salary. Competition is fierce in all of these occupations.

Strategy for Finding the Jobs

Strategies for finding the jobs include the following tactics:

1. Find contacts by joining professional theatrical associations and organizations.
2. Attend trade association meetings and conferences.
3. Learn as much as possible about every facet of theater. To get a foot in the door, volunteer.
4. Attend seminars, workshops, and courses in all aspects of theater, business, and fund-raising.
5. Look for a part-time or summer job working for a producer.
6. Contact theaters, production companies, colleges, universities, etc., to find internships, apprenticeships, and training programs in this end of the industry.
7. Offer to handle the fund-raising for your local community theater, arts council, or not-for-profit theater group. This will give you experience in raising money—a skill needed as a producer.
8. Try to find a mentor in theater who can help guide you in your career.

Prospective casting directors should be aware that it is almost impossible to get a job in casting without interning first. Many are willing to work free as a way to break into Hollywood, making competition for the jobs fierce. Find out about internships by looking in *The Casting Director Directory*, which is sold by Samuel French bookstore (samuelfrench.com). It lists the names, addresses, and phone numbers of casting directors and what shows they cast. Then send your résumé.

Potential theatrical press agents can acquire much needed experience by handling the publicity and promotion for a school, college, or community theater production. Look for seminars, workshops, and classes in publicity, writing, promotion, and theater. These experiences will improve your skills in addition to providing opportunities to make important contacts.

Professional Associations

Association of Theatrical Press Agents and Managers
1650 Broadway, Suite 700
New York, NY 10036
atpam.com

League of American Theaters and Producers
226 West 47th St.
New York, NY 10036
livebroadway.com

A Close-Up Look at Theater Business Professionals

Following are the accounts of four professionals who work in different aspects of the business side of theater.

Gary Murphy, Publicist

Gary Murphy is an independent publicist specializing in national public relations campaigns for the performing arts. He serves as the National Press Representative for The Geffen Playhouse in Los Angeles, the Alley Theater in Houston, and Santa Fe Stages in Santa Fe, New Mexico. He earned his B.S. in English education from SUNY at Cortland. Gary did not plan to enter his profession—it just sort of happened.

While Gary was recovering from an illness several years ago, a friend suggested that he tend the intermission bar at Manhattan Theater Club in New York. Although he had a teaching degree, he realized that he did not want to teach. Gary had no experience in theater, and never expected that he would end up making it his career. Working at the Manhattan Theater Club was just the beginning. As Gary says, "After that gig, I was hooked on theater. I proceeded to work in the box office, the marketing department, and then the press department, gaining my real theater schooling in a two-and-one-half-year paid apprenticeship at Manhattan Theater Club."

Following this introduction to theater, Gary next worked as Marketing and Press Director for Manhattan Punch Line (an independent publicist for a number of theater productions). From there he went to Circle Repertory Company as Communications Director from 1985 to 1991, and next to New York Theater Workshop as Press Representative from 1988 to 1991.

Working as an independent publicist guarantees Gary a very full schedule. Although his daily routine varies, it always includes a good deal of writing. Memos, faxes, press releases, photo identifications, and letters are a regular part of his job, regardless of whatever other activities demand his attention.

Gary maintains a database press list that he constantly updates. He tries to get daily news updates from clients about their projects, and looks for news that can be turned into press items. He also hires photographers for production shoots and works in conjunction with the managing directors of theaters.

One of Gary's primary responsibilities to his clients is to handle all opening nights. Coordinating these events involves inviting the press, creating press kits, and meeting and greeting all invited guests at the event. During October and November, the high season in theater, Gary can work up to sixty hours a week.

"What I enjoy the most is dealing with the artists and the media," Gary says. "I enjoy working with writers-playwrights as much as critics—and it gives me tremendous pleasure to bring a playwright's work to the attention of the media. I have been fortunate to work with some of the finest artists appearing on stage during the last twenty years, and I've also worked with a number of vital theater institutions responsible for keeping American theater moving forward. They include the Manhattan Theatre Club, Circle Repertory Company, New York Theatre Workshop, and currently The Geffen Playhouse."

Wayne Keller, Artists' Representative

Since most actors and performers need agents to find work, the job of artists' representative is very important in the business of theater. Wayne Keller works as an artists' representative in Nashville, Tennessee. He attended Michigan State University in East Lansing, where he majored in police administration and minored in communications.

"There is really no training ground or formal education for this profession," says Wayne. "You must first learn the business from its performing standpoint, then from the producer's or club owner's angle. I personally grew up in my father's nightclub in Milwaukee, learned the entertainer's standpoint by 'hanging around' with numerous talented performers, and by utilizing normal small business practices. My work history prior to becoming an agent was as an office manager for the Pinkerton Detective Agency."

Wayne's experience has helped him to define the qualities necessary for a beginning agent. He lists "honesty, availability, and the ability to tolerate and nurture the egos of the talented" as the most important qualities for anyone entering this field. Although he brought these same qualities to his work when he first became an agent, Wayne did not have one other attribute that he feels is also important. He believes that a successful agent should first be a performer, an experience that adds to the agent's ability to understand clients' needs.

Wayne describes his profession as unique in its workings. "You go out evenings to watch various people perform and endeavor to have a discussion with them. A few days, weeks, or months later, they write you (submitting photos), and advise you of their availability on a certain date. You then contact a producer or club owner and inform him or her of the availability and attributes of the entertainer. (One thing is for sure—there is never anything negative about a performer you are selling.) A contract for that one engagement is then prepared and you go on to the next booking."

Wayne says that once an agent becomes established and has won the confidence of clients, the business becomes somewhat routine. "You are the catalyst between the acts and their appearances. The atmosphere in the business is always very relaxed, and you reach a point where you are paid more for what you know than for the number of hours you work."

Those agents who attain national reputations and industry respect can leave the mechanics of drawing up contracts to assistants, and devote the majority of their time to securing more publicity for clients.

Wayne talks about the ups and downs of working as an agent. "The upsides of the business are numerous if you have the ability to do the job. You are constantly dealing with interesting, talented people and behind the scenes of a fascinating field. Your income is restricted only by your own ability. Your schedule is very adaptable, and you need only work the hours you choose.

"The downsides include producers and club owners who are not honest with you and do not pay you the agreed fees. And, to some extent, the aforementioned inflated ego of the performers. I must say in defense of these performer egos, however, that they are a necessity. If one is to get up before hundreds of people show after show, night after night, you have to believe in yourself, and if your agent chooses to call that an inflated ego it's his or her problem!"

Jennifer LaPorte, Fine Arts Manager

Jennifer LaPorte is the Fine Arts Manager at Alverno College in Milwaukee, Wisconsin. Her job is a combination of theater, business, and education.

Jennifer's background is in theater and teaching. Her goal was not to be a performer, but to work in an educational setting or in experimental theater. She began her career by teaching acting at a community center, where she eventually secured a job in a pregnancy prevention/teen mentoring program.

Jennifer describes what happened next: "When they found out that I could write well enough to crank out grant proposals and was willing to work erratic hours onstage, in the gallery, and in the office, I got the arts coordinator position. There I learned about fund-raising, programming, and marketing."

Jennifer offers a general description of her job, including the ups and downs of the work. "Arts administration is exciting because it encompasses programming, marketing fund development, and education," she says. "So it requires juggling quite a number of different tasks, all at the same time. You must always keep in mind that a lack of grant money could wipe out your job in one fell swoop even though you are working long, but meaningful hours.

"As the manager of a college's performing arts series, there are also duties related to curriculum connections and serving as a marketing tool for the college. There is a constant pressure to work over and beyond your job description because sometimes what you do is perceived as an 'extra' or 'fun.' However, most arts administrators take their work very seriously and do it for the love of the arts, not for the money (which isn't there anyway). Arts administrators sometimes also have to fight the perception that people in the arts are poor money managers and disorganized. Truth be told, you need to be incredibly organized. Creativity is important, but almost secondary to running a tight ship."

Advice from the Professionals

Gary Murphy shares some honest advice for theater majors. "Don't follow in my footsteps," he says. "Make your own way. There are no set rules, no set game plan. If you want to be an actor, designer, or director you can go to Julliard, Yale, or Northwestern University and receive some of the best training available. Academic programs are available in theater administration, and I'd recommend that you choose one that gives you a solid liberal arts/business education along with the theater background. But more than that, if you want to work in theater today, you just have to love it. It's that simple. Because when you love what you do, nothing is too much, and the learning never stops."

Wayne Keller has some advice for aspiring agents: "If someone is interested in becoming an agent, he or she should first acquire a working knowledge of show business and (1) be honest, and (2) always be available to his or her people. You must realize that you are responsible for the livelihood of these entertainers, and you must take care of them as your own.

"I was attracted to the business by a love of entertainment, a kind of fascination for the performers, and an awareness of income possibilities that superseded a career as a private detective. Also, in working for yourself you are totally in control of your own destiny in the business world. For me, this translated into thirty wonderful years in this career."

Jennifer LaPorte offers these thoughts about arts administration: "My advice is to volunteer as much as possible and to stay involved in other arts groups as well as the one you work for. And," she adds, "rather than pursuing a master's in arts administration, I'd recommend that you get as much experience on the job as possible."

9

Path 4: Teaching Theater

"[A teacher is] the man who can make hard things easy."
—Ralph Waldo Emerson

While knowledge is one barometer for measuring the effectiveness of a teacher, a number of other qualities are equally important. If you possess a genuine desire to educate people, are an able communicator, enjoy interacting with others, are highly motivated and organized, and have patience and a sense of humor, then you have the potential to be an outstanding teacher.

Though teaching offers much in the way of independence, financial security, and time off, it requires a large measure of hard work, both physically and mentally. But, for most, the returns are manifest in the form of the intrinsic rewards received knowing you have contributed to someone's future—indeed, perhaps the future for all of us.

Definition of the Career Path

Theater teachers instruct or coach students in the techniques of acting, directing, playwriting, script analysis, and the history of theater. They help students acquire confidence, assurance, speaking skills, and timing. They encourage students in their work, direct rehearsals, and guide pupils in their roles. At the same time, they instruct students in backstage work including set design, production organization, set building, stage lighting and sound, properties, costuming, and makeup.

At the high school level, theater may be a part of English or language arts classes. On the other hand, many high schools today have separate theater departments. They may offer classes in acting, directing, theater history, stage-craft, makeup, playwriting, wardrobe, speech arts, and theater management.

In most schools and colleges, theater teachers and administrators produce or direct plays for school and public performance. They audition students by cold reading of plays or listening to prepared auditions in order to judge the pupil's potential. Theater teachers also stress the front-of-the-house or management duties of a stage show. Students learn publicity and promotion, programs, tickets, ushering, and business procedures.

In general, college teachers are specialists in one or two theater arts. They may work in acting, which focuses on scenes, study, improvisation, voice for the actor, classical acting, and audition techniques. They may teach technical skills such as set construction, properties, lighting, sound, costume construction, and makeup. Some teach the art of directing, playwriting, or both. Others teach stage production and arts administration.

Theater teachers may lead seminars and workshops or arrange trips to professional plays or plays at other schools. They may work on drama forms such as mime, improvisation, and reader's theater. Some produce children's theater, summer theater, or dinner theater.

College teachers may also do research and write articles and books. They may take on projects such as plays written by students or young playwrights. Some develop programs that give theater experience to troubled children. Others work to present traveling street theater or community or regional theater productions.

School theater departments often give two or three full-length plays or musicals each year for the student body and the public. Theater teachers may guide students who give plays in local, regional, state, and national contests. School theater clubs may have ties to national groups.

Dramatic coaches work with actors in an attempt to improve their acting techniques. They conduct readings to evaluate actors' abilities and then instruct them on how to improve their performances. Areas of concern may be stage presence, character interpretation, voice projection, or dialect.

Possible Job Titles

Drama coach
High school drama teacher
Theater teacher
University professor

Possible Employers

Theater teachers work in almost every city and town. Most full-time theater teachers, however, work in or near large cities. They teach in public and private schools, colleges, and universities. Some work in regional theater, community theater, children's theater, or other groups that present theater productions.

A great many of these teachers are employed in some other capacity. They may, for instance, teach English, speech, and theater arts as an adjunct of this subject. Others may work part-time as directors of theater arts. Some theater teachers employed by a school district may work in several elementary schools, junior highs, or middle schools.

Related Occupations

The United States Department of Labor classifies theater teachers with stage directors, stage managers, producers, communications technicians, casting directors, motion picture directors, script supervisors, radio and television directors, and program assistants in radio and television. Other related careers include actors, actresses, narrators, and drama coaches. People interested in the theater might also explore the work of set designers, property managers, lighting specialists, wardrobe supervisors, or other technical workers.

Working Conditions

Theater teachers in some high schools may put on plays in an assembly hall or gym. Others produce plays in state-of-the-art theaters. A college theater arts department may have a separate building and theater for productions and classes.

Most teachers have summer vacations of two or three months off. They may then work in summer stock or travel to see plays.

High school theater teachers work the same hours as other teachers at this level. Some of these teachers also teach other subjects besides theater. When a play goes into production, their hours may extend into the afternoon, evening, and weekends.

Training and Qualifications

Most theater teachers who are employed at the college level graduate with either a master's or a doctoral degree in theater or visual and performing arts.

Those who plan to teach at the high school level must take courses in teaching methods, along with studies in drama. Some states offer certification in theater arts.

More than 1,500 colleges and universities in the United States offer undergraduate and graduate degrees in dramatic arts. Studies may include the techniques of acting; history of the theater; understanding lighting, scenery, and costumes; analyzing and creating roles; working with directing concepts and techniques; script study and rehearsal techniques; and lab sessions to gain experience.

College students may major in acting, child drama, directing, playwriting, theater design, theater education, stage technology, or theater management. A part of the training includes staging and acting in plays. To obtain a master of arts degree, students take the curriculum prescribed by the university and produce a thesis.

To get a master of fine arts degree, students take mandatory courses along with electives and do a creative project. They must also pass tests, both oral and written. Doctoral candidates take more course work, pass examinations, and write a dissertation on some aspect of the theater.

Certification and Unions

Theater teachers in public and private elementary or high schools need state certification. Certification demands a college degree, a stated number of credits in a major, and courses in teaching methods.

Many schoolteachers belong to a union. The two principal ones are the National Education Association of the United States and the American Federation of Teachers. These unions negotiate contract terms on pay, tenure, working conditions, and other issues. College and high school teachers can also join the National Association of Dramatic and Speech Arts.

High school teachers may join the Theatre Education Association, which works to support theater programs in the educational system and emphasizes the importance of theater arts in the learning process. The American Alliance for Theatre and Education consists of educators, artists, administrators, and others serving young people in professional and community youth theaters and theater educational programs.

The Association for Theatre in Higher Education is a group of 1,500 individuals and 500 organizations that foster the interaction and exchange of information among those engaged in theater research, performance, scholarship, and crafts. The association sets standards of excellence for organizations and individuals concerned with postsecondary theater training, production, and scholarship.

Earnings

In general, high school teachers are paid on a nine-month or ten-month contract. Yearly pay may range from a starting salary of about $25,000 to $70,000 after ten years of experience. Pay varies with the size of the city or town, the region of the country, and the number of years on the job. In most schools, where theater is an elective or extracurricular activity, teachers get a set amount along with their regular salary for leading the theater club or group and directing productions. This amount is generally between $2,000 and $5,000 per year.

In 2002, median annual earnings for secondary school teachers ranged from $39,810 to $44,340; the lowest 10 percent earned $24,960 to $29,850; the top 10 percent earned $62,890 to $68,530. According to the American Federation of Teachers, beginning teachers with a bachelor's degree earned an average of $30,719 in the 2001–2002 school year. Private school teachers generally earn less than public school teachers.

In 2002, more than half of all secondary school teachers belonged to unions that bargain with school systems over wages, hours, and other terms and conditions of employment. The two primary unions are the American Federation of Teachers and the National Education Association.

Teachers can boost their salary in a number of ways. In some schools, teachers receive extra pay for coaching sports and working with students in extracurricular activities. Getting a master's degree or national certification often results in a raise in pay, as does acting as a mentor. Some teachers earn extra income during the summer by teaching summer school or performing other jobs in the school system.

Earnings for college faculty vary according to rank and type of institution, geographic area, and field. According to a 2002–2003 survey by the American Association of University Professors, salaries for full-time faculty averaged $64,455. By rank, the average was $86,437 for professors, $61,732 for associate professors, $51,545 for assistant professors, $43,914 for lecturers, and $37,737 for instructors. Faculty in four-year institutions earn higher salaries, on average, than do those in two-year schools.

In 2002 through 2003, average faculty salaries in public institutions, $63,974, were lower than those in private independent institutions, $74,359, but higher than those in religiously affiliated private colleges and universities, $57,564. In fields with high-paying nonacademic alternatives—medicine, law, engineering, and business, among others—earnings exceed these averages. In others, such as the humanities and education, they are lower.

Many faculty members have significant earnings, in addition to their base salary, from consulting, teaching additional courses, research, writing for publication, or other employment. In addition, many college and university faculty enjoy some unique benefits, including access to campus facilities, tuition waivers for dependents, housing and travel allowances, and paid sabbatical leaves. Part-time faculty usually have fewer benefits than full-time faculty.

Career Outlook

Although the demand for live theater today is not strong enough to support the many who seek to enter the field, countless individuals sign up to study theater in high school or college. These hopefuls create a demand for theater curricula and theater teachers.

Overall, employment of postsecondary teachers is expected to grow much faster than the average for all occupations through 2012. A significant proportion of these new jobs will be part-time positions. Good job opportunities are expected as retirement of current postsecondary teachers and continued increases in student enrollment create numerous openings for teachers at all types of postsecondary institutions.

However, many postsecondary educational institutions receive a significant portion of their funding from state and local governments, and, over the early years of the projection period, tight state and local budgets will limit the ability of many schools to expand. Nevertheless, a significant number of openings also is expected to arise owing to the need to replace the large numbers of postsecondary teachers who are likely to retire over the next decade. Many postsecondary teachers were hired in the late 1960s and 1970s to teach the baby boomers, and they are expected to retire in growing numbers in the years ahead.

Strategy for Finding the Jobs

High school and college students should participate in theater activities such as school plays, community theater, dinner theater, children's theater, playhouses, and summer stock. Students should also make an effort to read and attend a substantial number of plays. They should talk to actors and actresses, stage crews, and all who help produce plays to gain insights into the world of theater.

When they graduate from college, most job seekers get help from school placement offices. Some colleges and universities offer graduates assistantships. Students may also check theater journals for job listings, auditions, and other leads. Some state, regional, and other theater groups have placement bureaus. Some associations have employment referral systems.

Professional Associations

American Alliance for Theatre and Education
7475 Wisconsin Ave., Suite 300A
Bethesda, MD 20814
aate.com

American Federation of Teachers
555 New Jersey Ave. NW
Washington, DC 20001
aft.org

American Theatre Works, Inc.
P.O. Box 519
Dorset, VT 05251
dorsettheaterfestival.com

Association for Theatre in Higher Education
P.O. Box 69
Downers Grove, IL 60615
athe.org

Educational Theatre Association
2343 Auburn Ave.
Cincinnati, OH 45219
edta.org

International Drama/Theatre and
  Education Association
http://educ.queensu.ca/~idea

National Association of Dramatic and
  Speech Arts, Inc.
P.O. Box 561
Grambling, LA 71245
nadsa.com

National Association of Schools of Theatre
11250 Roger Bacon Dr., Suite 21
Reston, VA 20190
nast.arts-accredit.org

National Education Association of the United States
1201 16th St. NW
Washington, DC 20036
nea.org

Theatre Communications Group
520 Eighth Ave.
New York, NY 10018
tcg.org

A Close-Up Look at Theater Teachers

Following are in-depth descriptions of the careers of five theater teachers.

Harris D. Smith, Associate Professor of Theatre Arts

Harris D. Smith is an Associate Professor of Theatre Arts at the University of Nebraska-Lincoln. He earned a B.A. in theater arts from Montana State University in Bozeman and an M.F.A. in theater arts (acting emphasis) from the University of Washington, Seattle. Harris is also certified by the Society of American Fight Directors (SAFD) as an actor/combatant in stage combat. He was trained by David Boushey (Fight Master and founder of the SAFD at the University of Washington—one of the few fight masters certified in both Britain and America), and is a member of the United Stuntmen's Association, Screen Actors Guild, and Actors' Equity Association.

Harris's professional work as an actor includes the films *Past Midnight, Amazing Grace and Chuck, Runaway Train, Seven Hours to Judgment,* and *Chips the War Dog,* the television miniseries "Pandora's Clock," and work as actor/stuntman on the X-Files interactive CD-ROM.

Harris began teaching in 1993 at the State University of New York at Albany. He planned to become a university professor, and had acted professionally for several years. His stage experience includes working with the Sacramento Theatre Company; A Contemporary Theatre (ACT; Seattle, Washington); Seattle Children's Theatre; and the St. Louis (Missouri) Black Repertory.

Harris describes his interest in acting: "I was attracted to the art of creating illusion," he says. "I feel that when drama is done well, in whatever genre, it can be very powerful, moving, even dangerous—dangerous not just physically but politically, morally, and emotionally. I get the most enjoyment out of seeing my students learn the skills needed to effectively create illusion.

"After teaching acting for a time, I found that I have a gift for sharing and teaching the art of illusion, particularly in stage combat. As a college football player, I understood the dangers of full contact in what some consider to be a violent sport. On stage, I have the chance to create that illusion of danger without bodily harm. I find this to be much more rewarding—and a lot healthier.

"Overall, I would say my athletic background and the aspect of sports as entertainment had the greatest influence on me. Besides, I love to perform."

Harris maintains a very busy schedule, based mostly on teaching and advising students. He usually teaches two classes each day, and assists on other projects in his department, including occasional acting in theatrical productions. He often works up to sixty hours a week, especially when he is involved with a production.

Harris loves his work, and cites the opportunity to work with gifted colleagues as inspiration for his own performance, both in the classroom and on the stage. As he says, "We share a common goal: to produce talented, well-rounded students in the arts."

Harris continues, "To me, teaching is one of the greatest jobs you can have. What I enjoy most is working with the students and pushing them to achieve beyond what they thought was possible. For example, about five weeks into one of my classes I require my students to perform a singing exercise. They may have to sing a capella. When they read the syllabus the first day of class I know they see that exercise and think 'No way.' After the performances, they are generally patting each other on the back and discussing how great and moving the songs were. It's so rewarding to see them take risks and achieve their goals. You can't put a price on that."

For Harris, the downside of the job is the more mundane aspect of the work. "My least favorite tasks include paperwork, grading, and other administrative tasks. I find grading to be particularly difficult—how do you grade someone on his or her life experiences, or lack thereof?"

Jana O'Keefe Bazzoni, Director of Undergraduate Programs in Communication Studies

Jana O'Keefe Bazzoni is Director of Undergraduate Programs in Communication Studies at Baruch College in New York. She earned her B.A., M.A., and Ph.D. in theater from City University of New York. She started teaching in 1975, and has taught full-time at Baruch since 1985. She is the author of a translation and commentary of *Natural Stories #1*, a play by Edoardo Sanguineti (Guernica, 1998) and coauthor of *Pirandello and Film* (University of Nebraska Press, 1995). Professor O'Keefe Bazzoni has published articles in numerous journals including *Business Communication Quarterly*, *Pirandello Studies*, and *Western European Stages* and given presentations on communication pedagogy as well as modern theater at national and international conferences. She also serves as co-president of the Pirandello Society of America and is editor of the society's newsletter.

"I like learning and helping others, and the variety, plus the various aspects of performance," she says. "Teaching combines these interests. When I began to study theater, at the age of ten, it was as a performer; later I became interested in directing, later still, in history and criticism. I have combined the teaching of speech communication, including business and intercultural communication, with research and writing in drama and theater."

As an Associate Professor of Speech, Jana did not teach specific theater courses. Rather, she used her theater training to teach performance techniques to students of communication. She spent two or three days in the classroom, time that she describes as "challenging and energizing, sometimes very rewarding and fulfilling, other times frustrating."

Jana's job also included administrative duties, such as managing advisement meetings with students, interviewing new majors, coordinating student internships, attending meetings, and interacting with faculty in other departments. As she says, "These are less public and exciting aspects of my daily grind but are equally challenging and never-ending."

Jana describes the ups and downs of the job: "What I like most about the job is my relative freedom to function independently, to change my courses and office management methods to suit the needs of students, current climates, and course content. I enjoy facilitating class discussions and managing the classroom in such a way that students become responsible for their own learning.

"What I like least is grading and the occasional problem of student misbehavior, for example dealing with someone who plagiarizes."

Steve Schrum, Assistant Professor of Theater and Communications

Steve Schrum is Assistant Professor of Theater and Communications at the University of Charleston, in Charleston, West Virginia. He has a B.A. in theater from Temple University in Philadelphia, an M.A. from Ohio State University in Columbus, and an A.B.D. in directing from the University of California at Berkeley.

Steve became interested in film in high school. By the time he was in college he wanted to become a TV/video director, and also worked in radio and theater. He ultimately realized that he enjoyed theater more than his other pursuits. As he says, "Part of it was working with actors over a longer period of time, rather than a quickie rehearsal before putting someone in front of a camera. Also, I preferred the live aspect of the performance, getting immediate feedback from the audience and using that to fuel the performance. As the years continue, I prefer the whole idea of collaboration with actors and designers who can take my basic ideas and flush them out to make more of them than any of us working alone could have created."

Steve's schedule is very busy, since he is always preparing for class, working on his classroom presentations, and preparing for rehearsals. During the semester, he is extremely busy when he is working on getting a show into production while still teaching.

On a typical day, Steve begins by checking his E-mail, which is how his students turn in assignments. He prepares for class and teaches. His evenings are often spent in rehearsals for upcoming productions. On days when he does not teach, Steve plans for the show or works on software for a class presentation. He also works on many outside projects, which take up varying amounts of his time. In general, Steve works ten hours a day, five days a week.

Steve says, "What I like most about my work is that, first of all, I am working and am doing not only what I was trained to do but what I enjoy most—directing and teaching (the latter also being an opportunity for performing for me). I also have a chance to direct whatever I want, which is great, and I have a measure of freedom to develop projects that bring computers and theater together. The university provides me with the hardware and software needed to do what I like to do."

What Steve likes least about his job is "the fact that I work hard on the productions and yet many people don't bother coming to the shows. However, the things I like the most outweigh the negatives."

Donald W. Guido, Technical Director, Department of Theater

Donald W. Guido is Technical Director of the Department of Theater at Binghamton University (State University of New York). He earned his B.A. in theater (design/technical concentration) at SUNY College at Oswego in Oswego, New York. Over the years, he has also taken several courses ranging from computers to theater safety, rigging, and rigging safety, to new products, in an effort to increase his job skills. The courses ranged from two-hour sessions to one that exceeded forty class hours. "The nature of life is that you have to keep on learning or you fall behind," he says. "A job in education requires that you not fall behind."

Donald's first job as a technical director was in 1975 at SUNY Cortland, a job he secured through contacts he made while a student at SUNY Oswego. He worked there for seven years, and in 1982 applied for and got the job of Technical Director at the Binghamton University Department of Theater.

"Theater (as in its related fields such as television, movies, theme parks, etc.) constantly creates new challenges," says Donald. "Perhaps it is the ever-changing nature of the performance arts that has attracted me to the field. I particularly like the fact that in live theater what we create exists in a moment in time and then is gone. Only the memory remains."

Donald describes himself as someone who "tinkers." He likes to take things apart to see how they work, an interest that he believes came from growing up with his father's home workshop. Building projects abounded during Donald's youth, and he worked a great deal with tools. He spent several summers as a maintenance worker at his high school and later worked for several youth programs and playgrounds.

Donald's initial college major was educational communication. He says that he joined the school's theater group "solely for social purposes. The group consisted of people who worked with tools, met regularly, and had access to a well-equipped shop. The fact that I was involved in theater was, initially, of no consequence to me."

Eventually, the theater group offered Donald a position working in summer stock at the Cortland Repertory Theater. He enjoyed the experience and realized that this was work that he could pursue as a career.

Donald's current position involves many different responsibilities. As technical director, he is responsible for the safe and accurate construction, installation, and removal of all the productions the Department of Theater produces.

A typical day for Donald is from 9 A.M. to 5:30 P.M. He might deliver a lecture, and will supervise a number of students in the scene shop. Depending on the classes being offered, Donald has between five and twenty students in the shop. He instructs them in tool procedures, safety, and construction techniques. Since most of the students have little if any experience with tools, they often require extra supervision. Safety is an important issue in the scene shop, given the number of tools and relative inexperience of the students.

Donald says, "There is also danger in the fact that we work in theaters that have grids up to sixty-five feet high. We work off ladders, vertical lifts, and cherry pickers. We fly scenery that can weigh just pounds or tons. We build scenery with moving wagons, slipstages, and turntables; then have students act, crew, install, and dismantle the sets."

Donald's duties vary depending on the show and the designer. Sometimes he gets complete working drawings, and other times he has to draft construction drawings himself. Some shows have straightforward sets from stock units, while others require sets built completely from scratch.

Here is a list of what a typical day for Donald might include:

Drafting
Ordering supplies
Tool upkeep and maintenance
Meetings
    Production related
    Department business
    University business
Lecturing to classes
Supervising work-study students
Supervising graduate assistants
Supervising students in shop
Supervising students in theater
Loading-in a set
Working on a set

Donald talks about the ups and downs of his job: "There is always an inflexible deadline and the tendency to cut corners. My job is to make sure the production remains on schedule, everyone works safely, everyone works carefully, that the corners being cut are not diminishing quality or safety, and that no one gets hurt.

"All of that said, I enjoy coming to work. I enjoy interacting with most of my coworkers and students. I like the fact that what we're doing each day is a little different from what we did the day before and from what we'll do tomorrow. I like working in the scene shop. I enjoy the challenges I have to meet to solve the problems of each show. I enjoy working with the rigging system, rigging shows. I feel extremely good about our students who go out and succeed in their chosen professions and hope perhaps, to some extent, I have assisted them on their journey. If that is so, then maybe I have repaid those who helped me on my journey. As some of my students go out and enter the same profession, we become references for each other, a support network that entwines us and our other contacts. Working on the shows becomes an important memory of college, and I enjoy being a part of that. After all, live theater should be an important memory in the minds of those involved in it—cast, crew, and audience."

Rick Davis, Associate Dean, College of Visual and Performing Arts

Rick Davis is Artistic Director of the Theater of the First Amendment and Associate Dean of the College of Visual and Performing Arts at George Mason University in Fairfax, Virginia. His education includes a B.A. in theater and drama from Lawrence University in Appleton, Wisconsin, and an M.F.A. in dramaturgy, dramatic literature, and criticism from the Yale School of Drama in New Haven, Connecticut.

Rick began working with Theater of the First Amendment in 1991 after spending six seasons at Center Stage in Baltimore. He explains why he made the move: "I was attracted to the program here at George Mason University because it combines a professional, Equity resident company with a liberal arts undergraduate theater program, an experiment I thought well worth undertaking, and quite a rare if not a unique combination. I was also at a point in my career (about eight years out of graduate school, a variety of experiences under my belt both in the professional theater and in academia) where I wanted to try my hand at running a theater and a theater program. TFA and GMU offered the chance to do both in a supportive environment."

Rick's interest in theater began early. He says that he has wanted to be involved with plays for as long as he can remember, whether that involvement meant writing, designing, directing, or, occasionally, acting. He first worked in a theater at about age ten, running the light board at a community theater.

Rick eventually majored in theater in college, and spent every summer working in some capacity in a theater, from directing to lighting design to janitorial work. He spent four summers in Colorado doing repertory stock, an experience that solidified his decision to make working in theater his career.

Rick's devotion to theater led to a rather brave undertaking right after finishing graduate school. He and some friends decided to start their own theater company. They raised money, handled publicity, looked for theater spaces, and chose plays, actors, and staff. The American Ibsen Theater opened in Pittsburgh in 1983. The company lasted for three seasons that Rick describes as "very interesting, critically successful, and challenging." Unfortunately, the theater members were not skilled at management, and their funding ran out. Despite the final outcome, Rick says, "I would not trade the experience of being in on the founding of a theater for anything. The level of commitment it requires is total, and the sense of emotional and artistic investment is profound. It shapes you forever."

During his time with the American Ibsen Theater, Rick was a faculty member at Washington College in Maryland, a position that provided both a steady income and an atmosphere that allowed for artistic and intellectual stimulation. Rick says that Washington College is where he learned how to teach.

When the American Ibsen Theater folded, Rick took a year-round position at Center Stage in Baltimore while continuing to teach at Washington College. He says, "Center Stage was an immersion in the world of the large, well-funded, and well-managed institutional theater—what a difference from the Ibsen Theater! Center Stage was and is artistically driven, but has sophisticated, mature leadership that recognizes how difficult it can be to be a 'grown-up' and maintain a theater career. They've taken steps to make sure that the things that drive people away from the business once they reach their thirties—burnout, low pay, poor benefits, a frenzied atmosphere—are brought under control to the largest extent possible. It was great for me to be a part of that for long enough to appreciate how it's done, and how important it is."

Describing a typical workday is a challenge for Rick, given the numerous responsibilities that come with directing a theater company and teaching. His work involves a good deal of variety and change, which is an asset for Rick. He describes some of his activities prior to giving this interview: "There is no typical day, but over the last couple of days this summer I've read a play for consideration for the season after next, interviewed a costume designer, spoken long-distance to the composer of our upcoming production about the vocal range of one of the parts, and to the director about what effect that will have on casting, talked to the set designer of the next play I'm directing, had four university committee meetings ranging from curriculum planning to marketing, proofread a brochure, worked on a press release, and given a lecture. All of that goes on pretty much all the time, and this is our quiet season. Once the school year and the theater season start, add directing, producing, and teaching to the list. It is busy, yes, but we strive to create an unhurried atmosphere in our work, one that is susceptible to humor, irony, and recognition of those moments when enough is enough. In general, I'd say that I look forward to coming to work every day."

Rick most enjoys directing plays and operas, which he does several times each year, both at the university and off campus. He also loves to teach, and feels that the two endeavors reinforce one another.

The only downside that Rick describes is common to many working situations. "In any institution, but especially in larger-size academic institutions, there are bureaucracies, traditions, procedures, and other ways of making it difficult to do one's work quickly and sensibly. In academia there is also an unnatural enthusiasm for committees. And there is tenure. And . . . and . . . but overall, a university can be a supportive and exciting place to work if you keep your eye on what works and don't get consumed by what doesn't. That is true in theaters as well."

Advice from the Professionals

Harris Smith has some words of advice for students who are considering becoming acting teachers: "I would encourage potential theater educators to pace yourselves. Students will suck up everything you have to offer—which is great. But you need to have a portion of yourself left over to bring home at night to give to your family, who love you more than anyone else. And what you have for them must be genuine—for they know better than anyone when you're acting."

Here is Jana O'Keefe Bazzoni's advice for anyone interested in pursuing a career in teaching: "I would advise people who want to teach to analyze why it is they think they want to enter this field and then decide whether they want to teach at the college and university level.

"If their choice is for this level, they must be prepared to undergo rigorous training in a discipline and to learn about teaching, doing research, and publishing entirely on their own. They must begin early to network, to find mentors who are appropriate for the discipline and their career path, and to do research, write, and find publishing outlets that their peers will find suitable.

"Finally, I would advise people to realize that the college and university culture is an organizational environment like any other and that they must learn the 'rules' of the culture in order to strategically communicate and flourish within it, both as classroom teachers and as productive scholars and members of the university community."

Steve Schrum's advice for newcomers to the field: "I would advise that candidates for this career do as much production work as you can in as many areas as you can to get as much practical experience as possible. For the academics, read as many plays as possible and try to make connections between everything. And don't let the semester-size lumps (as someone once called them) of theater history be all you know—do as much extra reading as possible to provide yourself with as extensive and comprehensive knowledge of theater as possible."

Speaking as a technical director, Donald Guido advises, "Pace yourself, there is a lot of burnout in this field. Be sure you enjoy all of this—it is a lot of work. Don't expect to get rich, the pay isn't great and the rewards are mostly personal. Don't let the job rule your personal life—and be sure you have a life outside the job. Don't ever forget that many people's safety and lives (both literally and figuratively) are in your hands—don't succumb to the pressure to do something unsafe. It is a great job, just don't let it control your existence. I'm still enjoying the ride."

Rick Davis offers some good advice for anyone thinking of a career in theater: "Realize that no scrap of experience or knowledge is ever wasted when one is pursuing a life in the theater. Be hungry for as much of both as you can handle. Read widely, listen to music (all kinds), look at lots of pictures, read the newspaper every single day. Cultivate collaborators in whom you have confidence and for whom you have enthusiasm. Have at least one thing you do outside the theater that is important and stimulating to you. Etymologize the word *liberal* as in liberal arts, and recognize that it's not exactly what most people think it is. Then pursue it."

10

Path 5:
Other Theater Careers

*"The absorption of the ideas by the characters, the dramatic or comic force
which the characters give to the ideas."*
—HENRY BECQUE

In addition to the various careers covered throughout this book, here are a few other possibilities for theater majors: drama therapist; playwright; screenwriter; radio and television announcer, broadcaster, or DJ; drama or theater critic.

Drama Therapist

Drama and other creative therapists usually work closely with a consultation team of medical professionals to treat and rehabilitate people with physical,

---

CASTING NOTICE

Correctional Medical Services, a pioneer in the correctional health-care industry, invites you to a unique and rewarding field for a Drama Therapist. We currently have full-time positions available in correctional mental health units in Newark, Trenton, Bridgeton, and Clinton (Cumberland Co.), NJ.

Our facilities use a collaborative multidisciplinary team approach. In this setting, you will be responsible for the planning and delivery of drama therapy programs as well as participate with the treatment team in the development and delivery of a comprehensive plan of care and treatment.

Candidates must be registered as a Drama Therapist and possess a master's degree in Drama Therapy.

We offer excellent benefits, including 401K retirement plan, five weeks paid time off in first complete year, tuition reimbursement, and more!

---

mental, and emotional disabilities. Using the creative processes inherent in drama, therapists conduct individual or group sessions to determine the underlying causes of some problems and to help patients achieve therapeutic goals.

Drama therapy is an active, experiential approach that facilitates the client's ability to tell his or her story, solve problems, set goals, express feelings appropriately, improve interpersonal skills and relationships, and strengthen the ability to perform personal life roles while increasing flexibility between roles.

This type of therapy has proven to be effective in treating a variety of conditions, including Alzheimer's disease, eating disorders, mental retardation, autism, and substance abuse and has also shown promise in treating the speech and hearing impaired.

Possible Employers

Possible employers for drama therapists might be hospitals, clinics, rehabilitation centers, children's homes, schools, nursing homes, and assisted living facilities.

Working Conditions

Most drama therapists work a forty-hour, five-day-a-week schedule with the possibility of overtime. The number of patients under a therapist's care at any one time depends on the specific employment setting. Some therapists maintain service contracts with several facilities. Many choose to be self-employed and work with patients in their own studios, building a private caseload of patients through consultation with a medical or rehabilitation team.

Drama therapists spend much of their time in pleasant recreation or activity rooms in clinical or community settings. They may be required to travel to various locations, maintain records, and meet with other professionals to discuss the progress of a client.

Training and Qualifications

Drama therapists are trained in theater arts, psychology, psychotherapy, and drama therapy. Areas of study include improvisation, puppetry, role-playing, mask work, pantomime, theatrical production, psychodrama, developmental psychology, theories of personality, and group process. All students of drama therapy must complete supervised clinical internships with a broad range of populations.

The National Association for Drama Therapy (NADT) has established standards of registration for those who wish to become registered drama therapists (RDTs). Standards of registration include a master's or doctoral degree in drama therapy from an NADT-approved approved college or university, and the completion of 500 hours of drama/theater experience and 1,000 hours of paid experience in drama therapy. The NADT currently recognizes programs at New York University, California Institute of Integral Studies in San Francisco, and Concordia University in Montreal.

Drama therapists must have artistic ability, an understanding and appreciation for theater, a good sense of humor, patience, tact, stamina, and the ability to build rapport with others. They must also adapt easily to changing circumstances, be able to handle disappointments, and display creativity, imagination, enthusiasm, and energy.

Earnings

Salaries and benefits vary according to educational background, experience, and geographical location. If employed full time, drama therapists usually receive health insurance, pension plans, paid holidays, and vacations. (Those who are self-employed are responsible for providing their own benefits.) Some employers may provide tuition assistance for further study.

Following are average salaries in the field:

Starting—$20, 000 to $30,000 per year
With experience—$25,000 to $40,000 per year
Administration/management—$35,000 to $50,000 per year
Government (GS 7 to GS 13)—$29,800 to $63,000 per year
(GS 7 = bachelor's degree, GS 9 = master's, GS 11 = supervisory, GS
    13 = management)

Career Outlook

Drama therapy as a career is growing very rapidly, and many new positions are created each year, though total numbers are still small. Job openings in facilities such as nursing homes should continue to gain in numbers as the elderly population grows. As a result of an increase in managed care facilities, chronic pain clinics and cancer care facilities are also beginning to hire therapists. Job growth is also expected in assisted living facilities, outpatient physical and psychiatric rehabilitation, and services for people with disabilities.

Professional Associations

American Society of Group Psychotherapy and
    Psychodrama (ASGPP)
301 N. Harrison St., Suite 508
Princeton, NJ 08540
asgpp.org

National Association for Drama Therapy, Inc.
15 Post Side Ln.
Pittsford, NY 14534
nadt.org

Playwright

Playwrights write original plays, such as tragedies, comedies, or dramas, or adapt themes from fictional, historical, or narrative sources for dramatic presentation. Sometimes a playwright writes a play and then attempts to locate a producer to finance it and put it into production. In other cases, a producer may have an idea and retain a playwright to develop the script.

For the playwright to write a script, he or she first develops an idea for a story. Many things must be considered before a playwright can begin composing a play. Will it be a comedy, mystery, thriller, or musical? Who will the characters be? What will they be like? What will the setting be? How will the story be told? What conflicts will the characters be involved in? What will the resolutions be? What will the climax of the play be? How will it end?

When a playwright creates a story, it must be written in a specific form for the theater. The script must be written in dialogue. Generally, a script indicates the dialogue that a character is supposed to speak. The lines are next to or under the individual character's name. The playwright must also include settings of scenes, and descriptions of the characters and the movements that a particular character must make.

The playwright's job is generally not completed even after the script is finished. A producer may ask the playwright to make changes at any time.

CASTING NOTICE: THE SEARCH FOR A PLAYWRIGHT

We are a new, energetic, working theater company based in New York City. With two shows in rehearsal for the New York Ribbon Festival, a play-reading series in the works, and the workshopping of a screenplay, we have been very busy. But more important than any of this is that we are searching for our next project! If you are a playwright and want to see your work produced in the big city, then please get in contact with us. We read every play in the hopes that it will be "the one." We are accepting scripts by mail only. Please send your submissions to: Triple Puppy Group, 345 87th Street, Suite 413, New York, NY. We look forward to hearing from you soon!

CASTING NOTICE : LAWRENCE THEATRE

14 Ballroom Street, Buffalo, NY Dramaturg: Les Wilson.
Produces four full-length, ten to fifteen short plays per year. Submit complete manuscript. Reports in six months. Buys first production rights. Pays 8 percent royalty plus travel and accommodations for opening.

Needs: "Theatrical" work as opposed to mainstream television.

Tips: Sees a trend toward women's issues.

On occasion, the producer may also request that the playwright be present at rehearsals so that additional changes can be made at that time.

Since playwrights often work by themselves, their day-to-day existence can become quite lonely. However, most prominent playwrights feel that seeing their ideas, stories, and innermost thoughts presented for all to see is enough to keep them going through the preliminary stages of creating something new.

Possible Employers

As noted previously, playwrights can write a script on speculation in hopes of finding a producer to finance the show. Others are lucky enough to have a producer contact them to write a script.

You'll find more opportunities in this field in culturally active cities. An aspiring playwright can look for a job as a playwright in residence at a repertory, community, or school theater. Individuals might also submit their scripts to producers who have not yet made a name for themselves, but are also trying to break into the business. Playwrights may also submit their scripts to community theaters, college theaters, and experimental theaters. These kinds of groups are often looking for new plays to present.

While many who want to can write a play, not everyone can create a good play and have it successfully produced. In all, there are not a large number of available jobs writing plays. Instead, most people striving to become successful playwrights have other jobs and write in their spare time.

Related Occupations

Article writer
Magazine writer
Novel writer
Screenwriter

Working Conditions

Playwrights usually spend their time writing in an office or wherever they are most comfortable creating. The career, for the most part, is a solitary one.

Training and Qualifications

While college will not guarantee success to a playwright, it is often useful. Colleges offering majors in theater, theater arts, scriptwriting, or acting often have programs through which aspiring playwrights can have their plays worked on, further developed, and produced at the school. This offers playwrights opportunities and experiences others might not have.

Seminars, courses, and workshops in all facets of writing, including scriptwriting as well as stage, theater, and acting, will be helpful in honing skills.

Reading can provide the foundation for your knowledge base as an aspiring playwright. Play anthologies provide a variety of styles and will help you get a feel for how characters are molded, layer by layer, word by word. Attend every show you can, whether local or Broadway productions. Don't take rejection of your work personally. Keep writing. Perseverance is a must.

The more writing experience a playwright can gain, the better. Writing skills and techniques need to be polished. Playwrights should have an excellent command of the English language and an ability to write dialogue effectively. They need to be creative and exciting and have the ability to bring stories to life. Entering writing contests (particularly playwriting contests) is an excellent way of getting noticed, and often these contests offer a staged reading or full production as their prize.

Playwrights must also be capable of marketing their plays. Once they are finished, it's wise to have them bound and copyrighted at the Copyright Office of the Library of Congress.

You can learn more about a career as a playwright by contacting the New Dramatists. This group can offer professional and business guidance in addition to offering a number of internship programs. Young Playwrights, Inc., is a professional theater company devoted solely to the work of writers aged eighteen or younger. It sponsors competitions, festivals, and conferences for young writers.

Earnings

There are a number of ways for a playwright to earn money. One possibility is to write a script and then sell it outright for an agreed upon sum of money. A playwright might also accept what is known as an option payment on a script. An option gives a producer the rights to the script for a specific period of time. During this period, the producer attempts to locate financing. If financing is obtained, the producer negotiates for the rights to use the script. Each time the script is performed, the playwright will then receive a royalty. This is similar to the way songwriters are paid for tunes they have written. Some playwrights have never earned a penny for their work, and others have earned millions over a period of many years.

Career Outlook

Only a small percentage of playwrights are able to sustain themselves full time in this career. However, there are a number of people who are able to get their plays produced by smaller community theaters and are waiting for reviews to build them a solid enough reputation to take them to writing off-Broadway plays and then to Broadway plays. The competition in this area is fierce, as it is for theater in general.

Professional Associations

New Dramatists
424 W. 44th St.
New York, NY 10003
newdramatists.org

Playwrights Guild of Canada
54 Wolseley St., 2nd Floor
Toronto, ON M5T 1A5
Canada
playwrightsguild.ca

Young Playwrights, Inc.
306 W. 38th St., Suite 300
New York, NY 10018
youngplaywrights.org

Screenwriter

Screenwriters create scripts designed for entertainment, education, training, and sales. Themes may be chosen by the screenwriters themselves (more common in television) or may emanate from a theme assigned by a producer or director (more common in films). Every television show or movie you see begins as a script written by a screenwriter.

College and other educational facilities offer screenwriting courses that will help you learn the craft of writing for television or film. There are also a number of books that will help guide you in the "rules" of format and structure in writing for television or film. A variety of guidebooks and reference materials is available from Samuel French, Inc. The company's website, samuelfrench.org, provides relevant links. In addition, Writer's Digest offers a wealth of information and resources at its website, writersdigest.com. Its annual publication, *Writer's Market*, is another helpful publication for screenwriters.

Possible Employers

If you already have a script written, you might want to send it to an agent. Before doing so, you would need to compose a cover letter telling him or her that you are interested in writing for television and would like representation. Indicate that you are enclosing a sample script. If the agent is interested in you, he or she will try to secure writing positions for you on various shows. To deal with television and motion picture people, you usually need to have an agent first.

Writer's Market provides information about finding agents and others who buy scripts. The information in the annual guide is also available online at writersmarket.com.

Working Conditions

Freelance writers can choose when and where to write. However, if you are lucky enough to find work and do not reside in Hollywood or New York City, you may need to travel before and after the production. Relocation is even a possibility.

Because there are also long periods of inactivity while trying to get projects chosen by studio executives or directors, most screenwriters have a second job in order to meet the cost of living.

While screenwriting is often solitary work, in some cases writers collaborate with one or more fellow writers on a particular project.

Training and Qualifications

There are no set educational requirements for screenwriters. A college degree is desirable, especially one in theater or liberal arts, which exposes the students to a wide range of subjects. Screenwriters must be able to create believable characters and build a story. They must possess a range of technical skills such as writing dialogue, creating plots, and doing research. Word processing and computer skills are also necessary.

Screenwriters must be persistent, patient, imaginative, creative, and skilled in negotiation techniques. They must also have the ability to tell a good story and possess expertise in verbal and written communications.

Earnings

Earnings for screenwriters depend on contract negotiations. Some writers receive a percentage of box office receipts. A beginning screenwriter might earn $50,000 or so for a project, while a well-established writer could command over $500,000. A screenwriter for a two-hour television movie might earn about $50,000, and a staff writer for a weekly program might earn around $5,000 per week.

Career Outlook

There is intense competition in the television and motion picture industries. As cable television expands, new opportunities may emerge. Television networks continue to need new episodes for long-running series. Demand should increase slightly in the next decade, but the number of screenwriters is growing at a faster rate. Writers will also find opportunities with advertising agencies, educational training, and training-video production houses.

Professional Association

American Screenwriters Association
269 South Beverly Dr., Suite 2600
Beverly Hills, CA 90212
asascreenwriters.com

Radio and Television Announcers, Broadcasters, and DJs

Announcers in radio and television perform a variety of tasks on and off the air. They announce station program information, such as program schedules and station breaks for commercials, or public service information, and they introduce and close programs. Announcers read prepared scripts or ad-lib commentary on the air, as they present news, sports, weather, time, and commercials. If a written script is required, they may do the research and writing. Announcers also interview guests and moderate panels or discussions. Some provide commentary for the audience during sporting events, at parades, and on other occasions. Announcers often are well known to radio and television audiences and may make promotional appearances and remote broadcasts for their stations.

Radio announcers often are called disc jockeys (DJs). Some disc jockeys specialize in one kind of music, announcing selections as they air them. Most DJs do not select much of the music they play (although they often did so in the past); instead, they follow schedules of commercials, talk, and music provided to them by management. While on the air, DJs comment on the music, weather, and traffic. They may take requests from listeners, interview guests, and manage listener contests.

Announcers at smaller stations may cover all of these areas and tend to have more off-air duties as well. They may operate the control board, monitor the transmitter, sell commercial time to advertisers, keep a log of the station's daily programming, and produce advertisements and other recorded material. Advances in technology make it possible for announcers to do some work previously performed by broadcast technicians. At many music stations, the announcer is simultaneously responsible for both announcing and operating the control board, which is used to broadcast programming, commercials, and public-service announcements according to the station's schedule.

Possible Job Titles

Broadcaster
Commentator
DJ
News announcer
Radio announcer
Television announcer

Related Occupations

A solid background in public speaking is the common thread that ties all of these careers together. Other positions that require these skills include salespeople, teachers, actors, voice-over specialists, public speakers, interpreters, and public relations specialists.

Training and Qualifications

Entry into this occupation is highly competitive. Formal training in broadcasting from a college or technical school (private broadcasting school) is valuable. Most announcers have a bachelor's degree in a major such as communications, broadcasting, or journalism. Station officials pay particular attention to taped auditions that show an applicant's delivery. In television, appearance and style on commercials, news, and interviews are also important. Those hired by television stations usually start out as production assistants, researchers, or reporters and are given an opportunity to move into announcing if they show an aptitude for "on-air" work. A beginner's chance of landing an on-air job is remote, except possibly at a small radio station, as a substitute for a familiar announcer, or on the late-night shift at a larger station. In radio, newcomers usually start out taping interviews and operating equipment.

Announcers usually begin at a station in a small community and, if they are qualified, may move to a better paying job in a large city. They also may advance by hosting a regular program as a disc jockey, sportscaster, or other specialist. Competition is particularly intense for employment by networks, and employers look for college graduates with at least several years of successful announcing experience.

Announcers must have a pleasant and well-controlled voice, good timing, excellent pronunciation, and correct grammar. College broadcasting programs offer courses, such as voice and diction, to help students improve their vocal qualities. Television announcers need a neat, pleasing appearance as well. Knowledge of theater, sports, music, business, politics, and other subjects likely to be covered in broadcasts improves one's chances for success. Announcers also must be computer literate because programming is created and edited by computer. Announcers need strong writing skills because they normally write their own material. In addition, they should be able to ad-lib all or part of a show and to work under tight deadlines. The most successful announcers attract a large audience by combining a pleasing personality and voice with an appealing style.

High school and college courses in English, public speaking, drama, foreign languages, and computer science are valuable, and hobbies such as sports and music are additional assets. Students may gain valuable experience at campus radio or TV facilities and at commercial stations while serving as interns. Paid or unpaid internships provide students with hands-on training and the chance to establish contacts in the industry. Unpaid interns often receive college credit and are allowed to observe and assist station employees. Although the Fair Labor Standards Act limits the work unpaid interns may perform in a station, unpaid internships are the rule. Unpaid internships sometimes lead to paid internships, which are valuable because interns do work ordinarily performed by regular employees and may even go on the air.

Students considering enrolling in a broadcasting school should contact personnel managers of radio and television stations, as well as broadcasting trade organizations, to determine the school's reputation for producing suitably trained candidates.

Earnings

Salaries in broadcasting vary widely, but generally are relatively low, except for announcers who work for large stations in major markets or for networks. Earnings are higher in television than in radio and higher in commercial than in public broadcasting.

Median hourly earnings of announcers in 2002 were $9.91. The middle 50 percent earned between $7.13 and $15.10. The lowest 10 percent earned less than $6.14, and the highest 10 percent earned more than $24.92. Median hourly earnings of announcers in 2002 were $9.86 in the radio and television broadcasting industry.

Career Outlook

Competition for jobs as announcers will be keen because the broadcasting field attracts many more job seekers than there are jobs. Small radio stations are more inclined to hire beginners, but the pay is low. Applicants who have completed internships or have related work experience usually receive preference for available positions. Because competition for ratings is so intense in major metropolitan areas, large stations will continue to seek announcers who have proved that they can attract and retain a sizable audience.

Announcers who are knowledgeable in business, consumer, and health news may have an advantage over others. While specialization is more common at large stations and the networks, many small stations also encourage it.

Employment of announcers is expected to decline through 2012, owing to the lack of growth of new radio and television stations and consolidation of existing stations, but some job openings will arise from the need to replace those who transfer to other kinds of work or leave the labor force. Some announcers leave the field because they cannot advance to better paying jobs. Changes in station ownership, format, and ratings frequently cause periods of unemployment for many announcers.

Increasing consolidation of radio and television stations, new technology, and the growth of alternative media sources, such as cable television and satellite radio, will contribute to the expected decline in employment of announcers. Consolidation in broadcasting may lead to an increased use of syndicated programming and programs originating outside a station's viewing or listening area. Digital technology is increasing the productivity of announcers, reducing the time required to edit material or perform other off-air technical and production work.

Professional Associations

North American Broadcasters Association
P.O. Box 500
Station A
Toronto, ON M5W 1EG
Canada
nabanet.com

National Association of Broadcasters
1771 N St. NW
Washington, DC 20036
nab.org

Drama or Theater Critic

Critics, in general, can have a serious impact on whether a play or other staged event will meet with real success, financial and otherwise. Drama critics are assigned the responsibility of viewing plays and writing their opinions of the performances.

Training and Qualifications

Newspapers, magazines, websites sites, and other forms of communication may employ drama critics. To get a foot in the door, contact a local publication and ask if you can review a dramatic event (even if you won't get paid for it). You need to begin to build "clips" (published articles). This is a possible way to work up to paid assignments, larger newspapers or magazines, or other types of publications.

Don't expect this to be a nine-to-five job. Drama critics may work evening and weekend hours and be faced with difficult deadlines.

Earnings

Though earnings will vary according to the location of the job, the following represent average salaries: Local newspaper, writing reviews—$15,000 minimum per year; local newspaper, with experience—$20,000 to $25,000 per year; major publication—$75,000 to $100,000 per year.

Career Outlook

It is fairly easy to do this kind of work on a part-time basis and difficult to find positions on a full-time basis.

Professional Associations

American Theatre Critics Association
c/o THEatre SERVICE
10508 Courageous Dr.
Indianapolis, IN 46238
americantheatrecritics.org

International Association of Theatre Critics
aict-iatc.org

Other Careers in Theater

If none of the careers described in the book appealed to you, other possibilities that theater majors might consider are singer, dancer, choreographer, stunt performer, model, mime, magician, or puppeteer. Whatever you decide—good luck!

Appendix A

Course Descriptions

The following is a description of many of the courses included in the theater program at the University of Illinois, Urbana-Champaign.

100. Practicum, I: Practical work in the design, construction, and handling of scenery, lighting, sound, properties, costumes, and makeup for public performance. A minimum of forty hours of production activity to be arranged for each credit hour. May be repeated to a maximum of 12 hours. Prerequisite: Consent of instructor required for nontheater majors.

101. Introduction to Theater Arts: Introduction to models of theater production, including approaches to playwriting, acting, design, directing, theater history, minority theater, plays by women, and the integration of these elements in theatrical production. Lectures, discussions, and attendance at three Department of Theater productions are required. 3 hours.

109. Dramatic Analysis: Introduction to the study of plays for theater practitioners employing analytical methods and plays from modern theater. Requires paper of project assignments for each play. Prerequisite: Consent of instructor for nontheater majors. 3 hours.

104. Introduction to Scenecraft: Introduction to stage scenecraft techniques: basic carpentry, rigging, and scene painting. Prerequisite: Enrollment limited to theater majors. 2 hours.

105. Introduction to Costume Technology: Introduction to stage costume design and technology: approach to design, basic costume skills, and craft techniques. Prerequisite: Enrollment limited to theater majors. 2 hours.

106. Introduction to Lighting Technology: Introduction to stage lighting design and practice: approach to lighting design, basic lighting technology, light plots, and instrument schedules. Practical experience on realized productions required. Prerequisite: Enrollment limited to theater majors only. 2 hours.

107. **Introduction to Stage Makeup:** Introduction to stage makeup techniques: basic makeup painting, practice in corrective, aging, and character makeup, and introduction to creating facial hair and wigs. Prerequisite: Enrollment limited to theater majors only. 2 hours.

125. **Graphic Skills:** Introduction to drawing, technical drafting, and model building for the theater. Drawing and drafting supplies are required. Prerequisite: Enrollment limited to theater majors only. 3 hours.

126. **Stage Mechanics, I:** Study of the methods of acting, with emphasis on basic acting techniques; role of character in relation to the play as a whole, the play's internal and emotional values, and their interpretation through voice and action. Some sections reserved for theater majors only. 4 hours.

170. **Fundamentals of Acting, I:** Study of the methods of acting, with emphasis on basic acting techniques; role of character in relation to the play as a whole, the play's internal and emotional values, and their interpretation through voice and action. Some sections reserved for theater majors only. 3 hours.

175. **Fundamentals of Acting, II:** Exploration and communication of experience through speech and action on the stage. Some sections reserved for theater majors only. Prerequisite: THEA 170. 3 hours.

203. **Theater of Black Experience:** Surveys the Black Theater Movement's history and literature, and studies dramatic works focused on the black experience through the rehearsal and performance of representative works of black dramatists. 3 hours. May be repeated to a maximum of 9 hours.

210. **Oral Interpretation:** Oral reading for understanding, appreciation, and communication. 3 hours.

211. **Introduction to Playwriting:** Practical course in writing for the stage, including a study of basic dramatic construction and the analysis of weekly writing assignments, focusing on structure, style, and imagination, and culminating in a final term project of a one-act play. Prerequisite: THEA 108 or consent of instructor. 3 hours.

212. **Introduction to Directing:** Practical course in directing for the stage, focusing on script analysis, script preparation, casting, staging techniques, and design strategies, culminating in a directorial concept presentation of a contemporary play. Prerequisite: THEA 108. 3 hours.

220. **Survey of Theatrical Design:** Survey of design elements in theatrical production including the function of scenery, costuming, lighting, and

sound in conveying directorial concepts, style, and dramatic meaning. Intended for students not concentrating on theatrical design, this course requires both theoretical and practical projects. Prerequisite: THEA 101, 108, and 261, or consent of instructor. 3 hours.

222. Scenic Design, I: Projects and lectures addressing basic technical and aesthetic skills of scene design. Prerequisite: Enrollment limited to theater majors; THEA 125. 3 hours.

223. Technical Direction: Studies in theater production organization and technical direction. Prerequisite: Enrollment limited to theater majors; THEA 104. 3 hours.

231. Introduction to Stage Lighting: Studio course analyzing current lighting practices and equipment by means of production-oriented assignments. 3 hours.

232. Advanced Lighting Design: Lighting design for the proscenium, arena, and thrust stage. Prerequisite: Enrollment limited to theater majors; THEA 231. 3 hours.

260. Intro Asian American Theater: Introduction to Asian American theatre, with emphasis on theater companies, actors, playwrights, and audiences, through the reading of major dramatic works, examining production histories, and viewing Asian American performances and film. Same as AAS 260. 3 hours.

261. Literature of Modern Theater: Introduction to the principal modes of dramatic expression from around 1870 to the present day. Prerequisite: Completion of campus Composition I general education requirement and THEA 108; or consent of instructor. 3 hours.

270. Relationships in Acting, I: Behavior in stage performance explored on the basis of the actor's relationship with self, with objects, and with other players; emphasizes analysis of playscript to discover action, environment, and relationships. Prerequisite: Some sections reserved for theater majors only; THEA 175; or consent of instructor. 3 hours.

271. Acting: Movement: Basic physical training for expressive body awareness and dynamics. Prerequisite: THEA 175 or consent of instructor. 2 hours.

275. Relationships in Acting, II: Beginning scene work with special emphasis on analysis of plays, roles, characterization, and application of skills learned through improvisation and relationships in acting. Prerequisite: Enrollment limited to theater majors; THEA 270. 3 hours.

276. Acting: Voice: Fundamentals of voice and speech production. Deals with the fundamental elements involved in vocal production and good clear speech. Through exercises, the vocal and speech mechanisms are developed and applied to the delivery of text. Prerequisite: Enrollment limited to theater majors only. 2 hours.

278. **Movement Fundamentals:** Exploration of theatrical movement through the use of Bartenieff Fundamentals focusing on integrating and developing the body's core muscle groups to facilitate fluid and efficient integration of movement. May be repeated to a maximum of 4 hours. Prerequisite: Limited to theater, music, dance performance majors; sophomore standing and above. 2 hours.

320. **Advanced Scene Design, I:** Advanced problems in scene design for non-proscenium theaters (Section A) and television, film, and industrial design (Section B). Cannot repeat a section already taken. Prerequisite: Enrollment limited to theater majors; THEA 226; or consent of instructor. 4 hours. May be repeated to a maximum of 8 hours if topics vary.

371. **Acting Studio I: Dynamics:** Development of movement and voice skills for actors. Prerequisite: Enrollment limited to theater majors; THEA 275; consent of chair of acting program; and concurrent registration in THEA 372, 373, and 374. 1 hour.

372. **Acting Studio I: Voice:** Concentrated training in standard stage speech for the stage and the International Phonetic Alphabet. Prerequisite: Enrollment limited to theater majors; THEA 275; consent of chair of acting program; and concurrent registration in THEA 371, 373, and 374. 2 hours.

373. **Acting Studio I: Movement:** Concentrated training in movement skills and mask characterization. Prerequisite: Enrollment limited to theater majors; THEA 275; consent of chair of acting program; and concurrent registration in THEA 371, 372, and 374. 2 hours.

374. **Acting Studio I: Acting:** Acting in realistic and naturalistic plays. A performance is given at the end of the term. Prerequisite: Enrollment limited to theater majors; THEA 275; consent of chair of acting program; and concurrent registration in THEA 371, 372, and 373. 3 hours.

375. **Acting Studio II: Dynamics:** Continuing development of movement and voice skills for actors. Prerequisite: Enrollment limited to theater majors; THEA 371, 372, 373, and 374; and concurrent registration in THEA 376, 377, and 378. 1 hour.

376. **Acting Studio II: Voice:** Continued training in standard speech for the stage and the International Phonetic Alphabet. Prerequisite: Enrollment limited to theater majors; THEA 371, 372, 373, and 374; and concurrent registration in THEA 375, 377, and 378. 2 hours.

377. Acting Studio II: Movement: Concentrated training in movement for the stage, body alignment, and awareness. Prerequisite: Enrollment limited to theater majors; THEA 371, 372, 373, and 374; and concurrent registration in THEA 375, 376, and 378. 2 hours.

378. Acting Studio II: Acting: Development of acting skills for musical theater including dance, singing, and the analysis of British and American musical theater materials. A performance is given at the end of the term. Prerequisite: Enrollment limited to theater majors; THEA 371, 372, 373, and 374; and concurrent registration in THEA 375, 376, and 377. 3 hours.

391. Individual Topics: Individual projects and problems. Prerequisite: Consent of instructor. 2 hours.

400. Practicum, II: Advanced practical work in acting; theater management; dramaturgy and directing; and the design, construction, and handling of scenery, lighting, sound, properties, costumes, and makeup for public performance. 1 to 3 hours. May be repeated to a maximum of 12 hours. Prerequisite: Enrollment limited to theater majors.

412. Rehearsal Techniques: Laboratory course exploring the interaction between directors and actors in the rehearsal process. 3 undergraduate hours. 4 graduate hours. Maximum of 9 undergraduate hours or 12 graduate hours. Prerequisite: THEA 212 or 270. 3 or 4 hours.

413. Creative Drama for Children: Study of the history, objectives, and techniques of creative dramatics for children; laboratory applications. Prerequisite: THEA 108, 261; and consent of instructor. 3 hours.

414. Theater for the Child Audience: Study of the history, objectives, and techniques of play production for the child audience; laboratory application. Prerequisite: Consent of instructor. 3 hours.

417. Leading Post-Perform Dialogue: Study of the history, processes, and methods of leading discussions with social issues theater audiences. Emphasis on the skills and techniques of facilitators/peer educators; artistic considerations; function and application of the dramaturg; and practical experience through facilitation of social issues theater dialogue. Prerequisite: Junior standing or above or consent of instructor. 4 hours.

418. Social Issues Theater: Research, writing, and production of original plays addressing selected health and social issues on the UIUC campus in cooperation with the Counseling and Health Center. Course emphasizes training in acting and in methods of peer education and discussion facilitation. Same as GWS 418. 3 undergraduate hours. 4 graduate hours.

Maximum of 6 undergraduate hours or 8 graduate hours. Repeat and graduate students will be required to develop additional projects.

420. Advanced Scene Design, II: Advanced problems in scene design for period and style plays (Section A) and development of professional portfolio (Section B). May be repeated to a maximum of 8 hours if topics vary. Cannot repeat a section already taken. Prerequisite: THEA 320 or consent of instructor. 4 hours.

421. Stage Electronics: Laboratory course to familiarize theater students with the components, current wiring practices, and control techniques of theatrical electrical and electronic systems. Lab fee required. Prerequisite: Enrollment limited to theater majors; THEA 106 and 125. 3 hours.

422. Stage Mechanics, III: Study in advanced scenery methods and materials, including advanced woodworking, plastic-craft, and rigging. Prerequisite: Enrollment limited to theater majors; THEA 126. 4 hours.

424. Stage Mechanics, IV: Advanced study in the design and construction of moving scenic elements. Prerequisite: Enrollment limited to theater majors; THEA 422. 2 hours.

425. Stage Drafting: Traditional and digital drafting techniques for scenic and lighting design and for technical production. Prerequisite: Enrollment limited to theater majors; THEA 125. 4 hours.

426. History of Décor: Historical and comparative survey of designs, motifs, and forms of décor in the West. Emphasis on the relation between research and design for the stage. Prerequisite: Enrollment limited to theater majors; THEA 222. 3 hours.

427. Scene Painting: Techniques and practice of scene painting; lab time required. Prerequisite: Consent of instructor. 2 hours.

428. Scene Rendering: Traditional and digital techniques for creating perspective rendering for the stage. Prerequisite: Consent of instructor.

429. Stage Mechanics, II: Examines newly accepted and developing techniques and materials used in constructing and rigging stage scenery with emphasis on metalworking. Prerequisite: Enrollment limited to theater majors; THEA 104. 4 hours.

431. Video Lighting and Production: Study and practical application of basic television techniques with primary emphasis on lighting. Trips will be made to local television stations as well as major studios in Chicago to meet with lighting directors. Cost of field trips will be paid by student. Prerequisite: Enrollment limited to theater majors; THEA 231 and 232. 3 hours.

432. Lighting for the Musical Stage: Emphasis on lighting design for musicals, opera, and music concerts. Field trips will be made to area productions. 3 undergraduate hours. 4 graduate hours. Cost of field trips will be paid by student. Prerequisite: Enrollment limited to theater majors; THEA 231 and 232.

433. Business of Lighting Design: Practical approach to working as a lighting designer in professional theater, including working in nontraditional spaces, regional theaters, touring shows, designing in foreign countries, working on new plays, the role of an assistant, and finding work and negotiating contracts. At least two field trips will be required. Prerequisite: Enrollment limited to theater majors; THEA 231, 232, and 432. 3 hours.

434. Sketching for Lighting Design: Development of sketching skills and techniques used to present and communicate lighting concepts in relation to stage productions. Emphasis placed upon quick sketches using pencils, colored pencils or charcoal, watercolors or pastels. 3 undergraduate hours. 4 graduate hours. Prerequisite: Enrollment limited to theater majors; THEA 231 and 232.

436. Lighting Alternative Spaces: Survey of theatrical lighting techniques in such nontraditional environments as private homes and museums with emphasis on theoretical and practical considerations of design. Course culminates in large-scale outdoor final project. Prerequisite: THEA 432 or consent of instructor for theater students; ARCH 241 and junior standing for Architecture students. LA 343 and junior standing for Landscape Architecture students. All other students, consent of instructor. 3 hours.

442. Costume Patterning: Methods of draping and drafting patterns for period theatrical costumes. 3 undergraduate hours. 4 graduate hours. Prerequisite: Consent of instructor.

444. Costume Draping: Development of patterns for theatrical costumes through advanced draping techniques. Extensive lab work culminating in draping and constructing six complete period costumes. Attendance at ten professional fitting sessions at the Krannert Center for the Performing Arts Costume Shop is required. Prerequisite: THEA 442. 4 hours.

445. Costume History and Design, I: Surveys theatrical costume and fashion of major periods; emphasizes relationships to styles of art and dramaturgy, social milieu, and production design. Prerequisite: Consent of instructor. 4 hours.

446. Costume History and Design, II: Continuation of THEA 445. Prerequisite: THEA 445 or equivalent. 4 hours.

447. Costume Rendering: Studio course in costume rendering techniques: analysis of costume figure, rendering of fabrics, exploration of various rendering media. Prerequisite: Enrollment limited to theater majors and consent of instructor. 3 undergraduate hours. 4 graduate hours.

449. Costume Fabrication: Explores, through design projects, the appropriateness of various fabrics for specific costumes determined by historical accuracy, style, and constructability. Prerequisite: THEA 445 and 446. 4 hours.

451. Stage Management: Studies in the principles and the craft of stage management. Prerequisite: Enrollment limited to theater majors; minimum of sophomore standing in a theater curriculum. 4 hours.

452. Theater Management: Introduction to the basic practices of theater and arts management with emphasis on facilities management, arts marketing, and financial planning in the performing arts. Prerequisite: Junior, senior, or graduate standing in theater. 3 undergraduate hours. 4 graduate hours.

453. Theatre Sound Technology: Exploration of audio production techniques and equipment, as related to theater sound. Related topics include acoustics, electronics, and music. Prerequisite: Enrollment limited to junior, senior, or graduate theater majors. 3 hours.

454. Sound Design: Introduction to sound reproduction, recording, and basic systems design as applied to the modern theater. Prerequisite: THEA 453. 3 hours.

456. Property Management and Design: Principles of stage property design, planning, and management. Prerequisite: Enrollment limited to theater majors; THEA 104. 2 hours.

457. Senior Projects in Design, I: Professional studio and independent projects for student designers specializing in stage scenery, lighting, or costume design. Prerequisite: Senior standing in theater; consent of instructor required for nontheater majors. 6 undergraduate hours.

458. Senior Projects in Design, II: Continuation of THEA 457. Prerequisite: Enrollment limited to theater majors; THEA 457. 6 undergraduate hours.

460. Multi-Ethnic Theater: Focuses on the history and aesthetics of African, Asian, African American, Asian American, Latino/Latina, and Native American plays and productions. Prerequisite: THEA 101. 4 hours.

461. History of Theater, I: History of the drama and theater of ancient Greece and Rome, the Middle Ages, and the Italian and English Renaissance. Prerequisite: THEA 108, 261; and junior, senior, or graduate standing. 4 hours.

462. History of Theater, II: History of the drama and theater of the Spanish Renaissance, seventeenth-century France, the English Restoration, the eighteenth and nineteenth centuries in Europe and America, and Asia. Prerequisite: THEA 461. 4 hours.

463. **American Theater History, I:** Survey of the development of American theater as a cultural, social, political, and economic institution from the colonial era to 1900. Prerequisite: Junior, senior, or graduate standing. 3 undergraduate hours. 4 graduate hours.

464. **American Theater History, II:** Survey of the development of American theater as a cultural, social, political, and economic institution from the late nineteenth century to the present. Prerequisite: Junior, senior, or graduate standing. 3 undergraduate hours. 4 graduate hours.

465. **Musical Theater History, I:** History of the American musical from its earliest forms, including ballad opera, extravaganza, minstrelsy, and operetta, to the development of the modern musical of the early twentieth century. Prerequisite: Junior, senior, or graduate standing. 4 hours.

466. **Musical Theater History, II:** History of the American musical in the twentieth century, studied through the contribution of the major composers, lyricists, and director/choreographers. Prerequisite: THEA 465. 4 hours.

467. **Contemporary Theatrical Forms:** Study of post–World War I theater, including the New Stagecraft, expressionism, Brecht and epic theater, theater of the absurd, and later developments. Prerequisite: THEA 108, 261; and junior, senior, or graduate standing. 3 undergraduate hours. 4 graduate hours.

479. **Preparation for Auditions:** Each actor, through extensive research, prepares a portfolio of audition pieces for the opportunities imminent before and after graduation for resident companies, commercial productions, and film, or professional graduate schools. Prerequisite: Enrollment limited to theater majors; THEA 375, 376, 377, 378. 2 hours.

490. **Professional Internship:** Professional work with an approved host theater or institution in an area related to the student's academic program; exposure to and participation in professional theater. Full documentation and approval of internship activities required. May be repeated in the same or subsequent terms as topics vary. Prerequisite: Junior, senior, or graduate standing in theater; consent of Internship Coordinator. 0 to 14 undergraduate hours, or 0 to 12 graduate hours.

505. **Proseminar in Theater Practice:** Orientation to production activity at the Krannert Center for the Performing Arts, review of contemporary theater practice in the United States, survey of methods in production

research, and selected projects in theater specialties. Prerequisite: Enrollment limited to theater majors. 4 hours.

550. Colloquium in Design and Theater Technology: Projects in design for the theater or in theater technology, including stage scenery, costuming, lighting, makeup, projections, and sound and stage systems. Some sections require a lab fee. Prerequisite: Enrollment limited to graduate students in theater design and technology. 4 or 8 hours. May be repeated to a maximum of 32 hours.

Appendix B

Additional Resources

Career Information Center, 8th Edition. Farmington Mills, MI: Thomson Gale, 2001.

The Handbook of Private Schools, 84th Edition. Boston: Porter Sargent, 2003.

Hawley, Casey Fitts, and Deborah Zemke. *100+ Winning Answers to the Toughest Interview Questions.* Hauppauge, NY: Barron's Educational Series, 2001.

Mauro, Lucia. *Careers for the Stagestruck and Other Dramatic Types, 2nd Edition.* Chicago: McGraw-Hill, 2004.

Peterson's Four-Year Colleges. Lawrenceville, NJ: Thomson Peterson, 2004.

Peterson's Two-Year Colleges. Lawrenceville, NJ: Thomson Peterson, 2004.

Peterson's Guide to Graduate Study. Lawrenceville, NJ: Thomson Peterson, 2004.

Peterson's Professional Degree Programs in the Visual and Performing Arts. Lawrenceville, NJ: Thomson Peterson, 2001.

Peterson's Internships. Lawrenceville, NJ: Thomson Peterson, 2002.

U.S. Department of Labor. *Dictionary of Occupational Titles 2003, 5th Edition.* Chicago, IL: VGM Career Books, 2003.

U.S. Department of Labor. *Occupational Outlook Handbook.* New York: McGraw-Hill, 2004.

VGM's Careers Encyclopedia. Lincolnwood, IL: VGM Career Books, 2001.

Index